# Living with Kindness.

# Living with Kindness.

## Pat Downing
### with Larry Downing

Cover design by: Dylann Rhea

ISBN: 9798865348702
For more information visit www.livingwithkindness.com

*To Pat.*
My loving wife, lover, teacher, and inspired writer who 22 years ago
had the courage to say yes to me.

And to all of you, on your kindness path, adding love in action to
your world everyday.

**Kind · ness**

noun

Love with its workboots on

## What Goes Around Comes Around

*"One act of kindness can go on and on and sometimes,*
*like a boomerang, come back to us at a time*
*when we need it the most."*
                                          Orly Wahba

Living with Kindness

There are many reasons why kindness enhances our lives. This week we're exploring the delightful reality that kindness we give out comes back to us in often unexpected ways.

Yes, it may seem a bit selfish to be kind to others, but few of us are kind for that reason. We're mostly kind because it feels good. Kindness is a natural human inclination.

But isn't it nice to know that the more we perform acts of kindness, the more kindness shows up in our lives?

In our culture, people say, "What goes around comes around." In recent years, more and more people talk about the Law of Attraction, which explains how the energy that we put out into the world goes out, gathers like energies, and returns to us.

We experience it as people showing up in our lives in ways that are similar to the ways that we showed up earlier.

I read a story once – not sure if it was true or not, but the point is well made.

A man - let's call him Eric – was enjoying his morning coffee in his local café. A stranger began a conversation with him and mentioned that he was thinking of moving.

He asked Eric, "What are people like here?"

"What are they like where you're living now?" Eric asked him.

"They are terrible," the man replied. "Everybody is grumpy. They ignore me and never offer help. I can hardly wait to leave."

"Well, that's just what you'll find here," Eric told him.

Some days later, while Eric was enjoying his morning coffee, a woman he had never seen before started a conversation about the town. She said, "I love this town and I'm thinking of moving here. What are people like here?"

He asked her, "What are they like in your town?"

She smiled and said, "Oh, they're wonderful. Everyone is so friendly and always looking out for each other."

"Well," he said. "That's exactly what you'll find here."

What we give does come back to us – not in the exact form, but with the same kind of energy.

**I try to remember, "Wherever I go, I take me with me."**

I ask myself, "Which me am I taking out today? Is it the stressed and grumpy me or the kind and mindful me?"

This can be fun.

The fun part is looking for more ways to express kindness in our daily lives and then noticing how other people are showing up for us

When I was a teenager, one summer I was a waitress in the Rail Restaurant in Pleasantville, New York. Of the three of us, I was the newbie, just learning how to be a waitress. Before the customers came in, we each had a bowl of the soup of the day, so we could tell people about it.

The owner and chef was Rocky. The other waitresses told me he was grumpy and hard to work with. Well, I loved his soups, and I told him every day how good they were. It was a genuine response – a simple act that came naturally to me. At home, my dad always thanked me or my mother for a good supper. Kindness was a learned habit.

At the Rail, three of us worked at lunch time, serving mostly local businessmen, and one of us worked at night, when fewer people came. My first night shift was overwhelming – an unfamiliar menu and no back-up as more people came in. One man ordered a steak, and I wrote down the wrong one, so when I served it, he was upset.

I took it back to Rocky, expecting him to be mad, but he was kind to me. He prepared the steak the customer wanted, and I was relieved that it was so easily fixed.

The next day, when I told the other waitresses what happened, they asked me if I had to pay for the wrong steak. They were surprised that Rocky had not charged me for my mistake, since he always charged them if they messed up. When I thought about it, I realized that I simply acknowledged him for being good at what he did. It had an impact on him that later flowed back to me.

**Small kindnesses matter.**

Larry is a friendly person. He greets people whenever he encounters them. In the grocery store, he compliments the woman arranging flowers for sale. He enters into conversation with the produce man, and he greets the check-out person with a friendly comment.

As a result, they are always glad to see him when he shows up. They respond in kind, and it is a pleasant experience for all of them.

Most of them are used to being ignored by customers. Even check-out people, who are face-to-face with people, are often not acknowledged. An exchange of money occurs with no other conversation.

So a simple act of kindness — a sincere compliment about her smile or a comment about what a busy day she is having – can cheer up her day.

**We all want to be acknowledged.**

Consider in what ways you can acknowledge someone you encounter today. It's important to be sincere. An insincere compliment, no matter how good it may seem to you, does not have the magic of one from your heart.

Be aware of how you're feeling and what energy you're taking out into the world.

For years, I was uncomfortable when I approached a homeless man on the street – not knowing how I could help. So it was easier to ignore him. This is a common response.

In the last few years, we have had the opportunity to get to know several folks without homes, as part of the Haywood Street Community in Asheville, NC. When I asked my new friends, "What is the hardest part of living on the street," I expected they would say it was not having a home, or not having easy access to a bathroom or a shower. Those things certainly present big challenges.

But what mattered most to several people was the daily experience of not being seen  or being seen and dismissed as if they did not exist.

Don't ever think that a small kindness does not matter. What seems small to you can uplift another person in ways you'll never know.

I invite you to be curious. Experiment.

Look for small ways to be kind – at home or when you go out. Then notice if more kindness is showing up in your life. It often does not come back to you from the people you were kind to. But your own energy does flow back to you.

What goes around really does come around.

We're grateful that you are on this journey with us.

With love from our hearts to yours,

*Pat and Larry*

## Let's Allow a Powerful Vision to Guide Us

*"Create a vision for the life you really want*
*and then work relentlessly towards making it a Reality"*
— Roy T. Bennett

Do you have a vision of a better world than the one you live in? With all the reasons why we appreciate our world, there are also many changes that would make it even better.

Having a clear vision of what that world would look like provides a foundation for our lives – a focus that inspires our actions.

It is easy – and understandable – to get so caught up in the emotions of what is unfolding in the world around us today that we lose perspective. We forget the bigger picture of the journey we are on.

Some of us have not thought about a long-term vision of where we are headed. Sometimes, even when we have a vision, we get discouraged when we experience a set-back. We may feel defeated – or angry at those who seem to work against us.

We are human, and it's okay – even healthy to feel those feelings. Let them run their course. Speak them out loud. Rant, cry, yell. Do whatever you need to do – preferably in a safe place with someone who supports you - or even when you're alone.

Take some time to nurture yourself. After the stress of the last several months, we all need to take a step back and ask, "What do I need right now.?"

Take time to tend to your needs.

Then, when you are ready, think about your vision of the world you want to live in.

Get a clear picture of what that looks like for you. Write it down, so you can return to it later.

Let that vision inspire a sense of purpose in you. Let your sense of purpose guide your next steps and fuel your commitment to keep moving forward.

Now, you are ready to ask, "What can I do in service of the Vision?"

Let the Vision guide you. What action can you take now, despite what is going on in the world around you?

As you move forward, remind yourself of your vision.

## Our Vision

Our vision is a world in which we live peacefully together with kindness and consideration for one another. We listen to others, so we can understand them rather than judge or condemn them because they have made different choices than we have.

In our vision, love and compassion are the driving force in our individual interactions with one another, in society as a whole and also in our government.

Love in action shows up as kindness in our personal encounters – with family and friends, but also with strangers. It is considering their needs as well as our own, and taking action to support them in whatever way we can – whether with a smile and kind word in passing or an offer of more help where it is needed.

We live in a compassionate society in which we come together to ensure that everyone's basic needs are met. No one is excluded or neglected or abused in any way. Everyone has access to health care and good education that will enable them to live a productive and fulfilling life. Everyone's human rights are protected. Our physical environment is protected from destruction and we enjoy and appreciate the beautiful world that sustains us.

Our compassionate government is an extension of our compassionate society. It is an expression of the will of the people to live in a world of love and kindness. It provides efficient means of delivering services that support the efforts of society to provide basic needs – housing, food, health care, education, opportunities for good jobs, access to enriching experiences – the arts, entertainment, creative expression – and protection of the environment.

This is our vision of the world we want to live in.

**We see this world emerging around us.**

We see it in the kindness of people we encounter daily. We see it in our community as people come together to support one another and to help those in need.

We see it in people whose political ideas are different from ours, and we realize that we are all connected by a desire for a world in which we feel safe and have our needs met.

That world is already emerging, despite what is happening politically. We can rise above the divisions of politics. We can find common ground on which we can work together to create in our local communities what we wish to see in the world.

We can continue and expand the ways in which we are already taking love out into our part of the world.

We can continue to take a stand on issues that we care about, but we can do it without hating those who disagree with us. There's already too much hate in this world, so let's not contribute to the toxic mix.

Let's call upon ourselves to rise to a higher place. Let's remember our kinship with one another and let our actions be powered by love.

When enough of us make that choice, we will see our vision showing up in the world around us, and we'll all be uplifted by the fruits of our commitment to one another and to the world we love.

We're grateful that you are on this journey with us.

With love from our hearts to yours,

*Pat and Larry*

## Putting Judgment on Hold

*"It's not things that upset us, it's our judgment*
*about things."*

... Epictetus

The key is to find ways to see people and accept them as they are.

Sometimes daily interactions can be annoying – a rude comment can trigger a negative feeling. It's easy to take offense.

How do we get past our judgment and respond with kindness?

It's all about the meaning we give to it. We can take offense – or we can choose to see it in a different way.

## Shift to Understanding

I heard years ago that the person who takes offense is adding as much negativity to the world as the person who gives offense. That inspired me to look at myself and accept responsibility for my reactions to others.

As I considered my behavior, I realized that I often felt offended by a casual comment that could easily be ignored. Something inside me said, "How dare you speak to me that way."

Looking back now, I see how easily I was triggered to annoyance. My reaction was about me. I was reacting to the meaning I was giving to the incident, without knowing the circumstances or the intention of the person I felt offended by.

I now understand that the person being rude is probably having a bad day or a life that is daily much more challenging than the one I get to live. I do not know any of the circumstances of their life, but I don't need to know. I can give them space to over-react by not taking it personally.

Rather than reacting, we could decide not to respond at all, or perhaps a simple kind word would diffuse the situation "You are really busy today," may bring a smile of relief that someone noticed she was feeling overwhelmed.

Our judgment often shows up when we encounter someone whose life path has been different from our own, and we judge them based on what we would do – with the disadvantage of the limited perspective from our life experiences. We see someone living on the street and it's easy to judge them. I've heard people say, "They're lazy" or "They're losers" or "Why don't they pull themselves up by their bootstraps."

How much would it take to stop and realize that they may not have any bootstraps to pull up? They probably don't have the resources that we have – not just the physical resources, but also the inner resilience that comes from our life experience and the support of family, friends and community.

When given the opportunity, the most compassionate thing we can do is just listen. You might find a gift in hearing other people's stories. It will open doors to understanding. When we know about someone's life experience, we gain insights into their current reactions to life.

Like every aspect of our kindness journey, this takes self-awareness and a clear intention to move back from judgment of others.

My self-awareness began years ago with help from my teenage daughter. We had been in a store together, and as I was checking out, the cashier said something that triggered me. I overreacted. As we went to our car, I noticed that Christie was acting uncomfortable. When I asked her what was wrong, she told me that she had been embarrassed by the way I had reacted.

That was my wake-up call. I thought about the way I interacted with others, and I made a conscious effort to change to a kinder way of being in the world. It takes practice, and we get better at it as we go.

As Father Greg Boyle wrote,

> *"When judgment ceases to pull all the oxygen out of the*
> *room,*
> *an astonishing love takes its place."*

That is the goal that I am reaching for -- not nearly there yet but making progress.

We're grateful that you are on this journey with us.

With love from our hearts to yours,

*Pat and Larry*

## The Power of Your Thoughts and Words

"What we speak
becomes the house we live in."
… Hafiz

The thoughts we think and the words we say - to ourselves and to others - affect our feelings about the people who show up in our lives.

How do we let go of thoughts that prevent us from connecting with others?

### Start to Notice What You Are Thinking

We've talked about putting our judgments on hold, and that takes practice. It is all about noticing what we are thinking, then finding a different way of looking at the other person.

For someone we encounter on the street who appears to be homeless, we can realize that we don't know enough about their life experience to hold negative judgments about them. We can respond with kindness- even a smile and pleasant greeting is a way of saying, "I see you and acknowledge you." That is a gift more powerful than you may realize.

The energy we take with us when we're out in the world is important, but now let's think about kindness in our families and with our friends. These relationships can be challenging and often trigger us in ways that make it more difficult to be kind.

If someone holds different views than you do, and tries to persuade you to agree with him, it's easy to become angry and to argue. If a loved one is short-tempered or impatient with you, it feels natural to respond in kind.

When anyone triggers you to a negative reaction, this is your point of decision.

Can you see the situation from a positive perspective? Can you accept the other person's ideas as true for them and decline to argue?

Can you shift to seeing your short-tempered loved one as having a bad day and needing some love?

I once heard some guidance on how to decide what to say in any situation. The advice was to ask yourself if the words you want to say are:

> True
>
> Beneficial
>
> Necessary

Wow! That asks a lot of us.

It requires us to carefully consider what we're about to say. Not easy to do in the heat of the moment – but afterwards, we can take some quiet time to reflect on our interaction. That will enable us to set an intention to be more mindful of how we are responding to any situation that arises in the future.

This is a big subject that requires a deeper discussion, but now, it is food for thought.

### Be Aware of the Words You Are Saying to others

Once you have decided to shift your thinking about your response to someone, you also need to monitor the words you say to others about that person. Words have power.

When someone asks you how things are going, it's easy to complain about the person and talk about how badly they behaved. If you do, you will experience the negative energy you felt at the time of your last encounter and you will spread that energy with your words.

Why not talk about a pleasant memory or a time when you acted with kindness and the person responded in kind. You will be doing yourself and your friend a favor – and the other person, too.

Your words carry energy, and they affect you as well as anyone who hears them. What energy do you want to carry within you and put out in the world?

Be patient with yourself. This takes practice. But first it takes awareness. We start by noticing our own thoughts and feelings and how we express them. Then we notice the response of others to what we say to them.

That gives us the insights to support us as we shift to a more positive way of being with others.

When I first began noticing my reactions, I was amazed at how much negativity I was adding to my interactions with others. That was a big incentive to change myself.

It has been a long process. I'm still working on this. I still catch myself reacting with annoyance or impatience from time to time, but I am doing better now than I used to do.

Our automatic reactions are habitual. Changing them takes time and a desire to change how we interact with others.

It is a journey. We take one step at a time as we're changing a habit. Notice how much better you feel when you bring kindness rather than annoyance with you when you interact with loved ones or other people you meet in your daily life

Our thoughts and words determine how we feel, how we respond to others and how they respond to us. As Hafiz said, our words do become the house we live in.

We're grateful that you are on this journey with us.

With love from our hearts to yours

*Pat and Larry*

## Be Kind to Yourself

*"Almost everything will work again if you unplug it for a few minutes,  including you."*

... Anne Lamot

With everything going on in the world right now, it is so easy to feel overwhelmed. When we find ourselves feeling scattered, going in too many directions at once, we need to take time to get centered and focused.

This is the time to be kind to yourself.

Here are a few ideas that might help. Try one or two and see if you feel more relaxed and balanced.

### Create Rituals that Support You

If you spend quiet time every day to reflect on your life, you have a daily ritual. Perhaps you have a daily practice of prayer and meditation, or you set time aside to read something uplifting.

For some people, a morning cup of coffee is a ritual - alone or with a loved one.

Larry and I begin our morning with breakfast, then use our coffee and tea time to be present with each other – talking about any dreams we had or interesting ideas we read, often sharing uplifting quotes that trigger discussion about the things that matter to us.

This became a morning ritual – a time to connect with each other and with the loving, wise power within that guides our lives. We now begin every day feeling focused and excited about taking whatever steps the day holds for us.

Rituals can take many forms. The important thing is that they support you, uplift you and give you a sense of peace.

### Do Something You Enjoy Every Day

You might connect with a friend and have a little adventure or just a heart-to-heart conversation.

You may also be nourished by time to yourself. It might be as simple as a book by your bed that you read at night or a TV show that makes you laugh. You can play music you enjoy when you take a quiet break - or as you're doing your daily chores.

Think about activities that give you pleasure. Then be sure to incorporate some of them into your life now.

### Keep a Journal

A journal provides you a way to reflect on your day and make sense of all that happened. By recording your interactions with others, you have a way to acknowledge yourself for things that went well and to think about those that didn't. Then you can set an intention for tomorrow and ask your inner wisdom to guide you to a better approach next time.

### Spend Some Relaxing Time with a Loved One

It is so easy to get caught up in the demands of the day that we often don't spend time with those we love. By making that a priority – even if it is for 15 minutes at a time – we can nurture ourselves and also lift the mood of everyone involved.

### Take Care of Your Health

You know what to do. Be kind enough to yourself to do it.

### Laugh Every Day

Few things are as transforming as laughter. Studies have shown that laughter contributes to the healing of physical illness. It can certainly lighten a gloomy day and improve our emotional health as well.

Think about things that make you laugh, then make a point to include at least one in your life every day.

### Listen to Your Favorite Music

Music has the power to shift our mood. It can be energizing or relaxing, depending on our needs.

Sometimes, just having music playing in the background as we go about our activities can turn a chore into a pleasant break. When we need a time-out, the right selection of music can relax us or uplift our mood.

Music also comes with a second benefit. It can get us moving – even dancing – with its compelling rhythm.

When we care for ourselves, we feel more balanced and centered. Then, we are able to take the best of who we are out into the world.

We're grateful that you are on this journey with us.

With love from our hearts to yours,

*Pat and Larry*

# The Power of Gratitude in Challenging Times

*Gratefulness is the key to joy*
Brother David Steindl-Rast

Holidays are times of celebration and gathering with family and friends. At this time in our world, when social distancing is recommended, we need to find ways to celebrate while keeping ourselves and our loved ones safe.

For many of us, this means giving up the comfort and joy of family gatherings. It turns our holiday expectations upside down. We feel a sense of loss.

So how do we support ourselves and our loved ones through this unusual holiday season?

As in every situation in our lives, what we focus on determines our experience. If we continue to think about what we can't change, we can become overwhelmed by sadness.

This is an opportunity to nurture ourselves – to be at peace with what we have, and even to find joy, in this unexpected time.

Our first step is to stop resisting what we cannot change. That means not thinking about it, not letting our regret of what we have lost determine how we feel.

Then, we need to replace those thoughts with others that support us and help us to get back to a place of inner peace.

### Gratitude is the Key

We all have so many things in our lives that we take for granted.

This morning, I read a FaceBook post from a friend, Amy Cantrell, who has spent most of her adult life working to provide help and support for our homeless neighbors. She was out the other night doing street outreach - taking insulated tents, sleeping bags and warming supplies to people living on the street or in open spaces around Asheville.

She met a man on the street with all of his belongings in a grocery cart.

"Imagine picking from your life, from all your special things only what will fit in the basket. Imagine you are ushered from your home. You are homeless on the streets now.

"Your cart is now a lifesaver, always with you. In the basket, your coat, sleeping bag, a few clothes and toiletries. If you are lucky, you may have some old family photos that you must desperately protect against rain and snow."

Her words, as usual, went right to my heart. Sadness welled up in me, thinking of all our brothers and sisters without homes, then gratitude followed, as I considered the many blessings in our lives.

I thought about all the comforts of our life – a warm home with running hot and cold water, electricity, comfortable furniture, wifi, and the many amenities that add comfort to our daily life.

I thought about our family, with whom we won't spend Christmas or family birthdays this year, but who are a part of our lives, with love and genuine caring.

I said a prayer of gratitude for the blessings of our life.

Larry and I talked about our kinship with the homeless folks living among us and we said a prayer for their safety and protection. But there is so much more that we can do – need to do – to address this failure in our society.

**We can make a difference.**

Until we create a solution, the least we can do is to support organizations that are providing support now.

Several churches in Asheville provide food and clothing. Others also do outreach to take needed supplies for those living on the street or in open areas around town. If you would like to support their efforts, here are some of the organizations distributing life-supporting supplies to people living outside during these cold nights:

BeLoved Community

Haywood Street Community

ABCCM Homeless Services

If you are not in this area, it is easy to find the organizations in your community providing these services.

Let's celebrate this season by focusing on gratitude for our many blessings.

Then let's allow our gratitude to overflow by sharing what we have with those whose lives are more challenged than ours. A gift of any size will make a difference in someone's life, and in yours.

Now that's a celebration of the season, and a way to bring joy into our holiday.

We're grateful that you are on this journey with us.

With love from our hearts to yours,

*Pat and Larry*

# The Power of a Name

*Names are the sweetest and most important sound
in any language.*
Dale Carnegie

**I Have a Name**

My name is my claim to a place in this world.

My name is sacred. It carries my identity and my heritage.

My name declares my presence as a worthy member of the
human family.

It speaks of the unique gifts that I brought with me

when I emerged from the mystery which is my source.

When you say my name, you validate my existence.

You honor my uniqueness.

You welcome me into your life.

**Honoring Each Person that We Meet**

Asking someone's name is a way of acknowledging them. A
nurse who takes care of you in the doctor's office. A check out
person in a store. A stranger who is kind to you.

Some of us are not good at remembering names, but it's easy
to say, "It's good to see you again." That greeting acknowledges
them. Then, often I will say, "Please remind me of your name."
For me, it may take two or three times. That's okay. People will
appreciate that you want to remember their name.

Larry has an easy way of connecting with people. He learns
their names, and, after several encounters, he also hears some of
their stories. Once a connection is made, people sense who they
can open up to.

In the grocery store, he greets several of the regular staff by
name, and they respond in kind. He often compliments the woman
who arranges the flowers for the attractive display she created, and
he greets others with a comment of appreciation.

That is easy for most of us, but we often don't take the time to
acknowledge the people we see working around us. Knowing their

name strengthens the connection and the pleasure of the encounter for both of us.

Connecting with people we don't normally encounter in our daily lives may be even more rewarding. We learned this as we began meeting men and women who were experiencing homelessness.

When we first became a part of the Haywood Street Community in Asheville, we discovered an unexpected sense of kinship. We were in a place where all were welcomed and recognized as having value.

When eating a meal at the Welcome Table, we introduced ourselves and learned each person's name. It was a way to declare our presence and to welcome theirs.

As we sat at a table together and shared food, sometimes there was not much conversation. A simple inquiry of "How are you doing?" might open the door to further conversation."Where did you sleep last night?" often led to a response that brought the reality of their daily life home to us in a powerful way.

Many became friends– not just another stranger among many, but an individual with a life story and often deep wounds that they did not talk about. Those who did not speak much knew that we recognized them and cared enough to know their name. Even a smile and a greeting across the table is a connection – and it welcomes people into your day.

**We all have a place in the world.**

Let's practice the kindness of greeting each other by name. When we see others whom we have not yet met, let's remember that they, too, have a name, and they also belong here.

This takes us one step closer to the world we all want to live in.

We're grateful that you are on this journey with us.
With love from our hearts to yours,
*Pat and Larry*

# Changing to a Culture of Kindness

*Change is brought about*
*because ordinary people do extraordinary things.*
Barack Obama

We are in a time of dramatic change on Planet Earth. Many people believe that change happens outside of us, that we are pawns being moved around by some immutable fate that determines our lives.

We see it differently. We know that many things are out of our control, but we also know that we all have the power to help create the future that we want. We are more powerful than we realize.

We want to live in a world where love and kindness power the choices that people make. In order to help create that reality, we know that we must make it true in our lives.

## Change Begins with Us

*Be the change you wish to see in the world.*

Mahatma Gandhi

Living with kindness is a choice that we make, that enriches our lives and uplifts those we meet. Once we realize how much our acts of kindness uplift us, as well, we may realize that we have made a commitment to walk a kindness path, to be open to opportunities to be kind, and to plant seeds of kindness where we may not ever see how they grow in the lives of other people.

On the kindness path, we realize our connection to others, and we make an effort to rise above the judgments that separate us. We intend to see others in a deeper way, recognizing our kinship. That leads us to curiosity about them, wanting to understand them and to find ways to feel more connected.

Life often provides opportunities for us to step out of our comfort zone and to be kind to people whom we had overlooked previously. When we have the courage to take that step, we feel empowered, and we are more likely to continue to expand the reach of our kindness in other ways as well.

By choosing to live with kindness, we also invite compassion to accompany us on our journey. As we connect with others in a kind way, we develop an awareness of their challenges or misfortunes, and we want to brighten their day and to help in any way that we can.

Now, we can see how much Kindness has changed us and the way that we live in the world.

## Creating a Worldwide Kindness Movement

*People who are crazy enough to think they can change the world*

*are the ones who do.*

Steve Jobs

The choices that we make for our lives do make a difference in the world, whether we realize it or not. When we choose to live with kindness, we become the change we want to see in the world, and we help to bring about a kinder world.

When we join with others who have made a similar commitment in their lives, we exponentially expand our impact. Many individuals and organizations in the world today have large networks of like-minded and like-hearted people who are inspired to increase their kindness practice and make a difference in their communities.

The next step is to bring all of these networks together into a worldwide web of love in action. The more we combine our energies, the more powerful we become.

Let's look at just a few of the love-powered networks already making a difference in the world.

## The Revolutionary Love Project

Valarie Kaur, founder of The Revolutionary Love Project, gives us an empowering way to see what is happening in the world today. She asks us to consider: Is what we are experiencing "the darkness of the tomb or the darkness of the womb."

We like the analogy of the womb. As the time of birth approaches, the mother reaches a point of intense pain, with contractions coming rapidly, one after another. The technical term for that part of the birth process is transition.

If we can see the transition that we are going through now on earth as the birth of a new world, we can reframe how we view our lives. When the outer circumstances seem overwhelming, we can stop, take a few deep breaths to get our balance back, then push - take whatever action we are called to take in support of the emerging world we choose to create.

## Life Vest Inside

Life Vest Inside is a non-profit organization dedicated to inspiring, empowering and educating people of all backgrounds to lead a life of kindness while growing Kind Leaders of tomorrow.

Life Vest Inside has created a powerful kindness network that fosters dialogue with people across the globe, including parts of the world torn apart by conflict.

The success of "Kindness Boomerang", a powerful viral video with a message of kindness, encouraged founder Orly Wahba to build an organization that inspires people, especially children, to live lives of kindness.

## ServiceSpace

Nipun Mehta is the founder of ServiceSpace, which is "an incubator of projects that work at the intersection of volunteerism, technology, and gift-economy." Started as an experiment with four friends in the Silicon Valley, ServiceSpace has delivered millions of dollars in service for free to and provided by its over 400,000 members.

## Homeboy Industries

After several years as pastor of the poorest Catholic church in Los Angeles, California, Father Boyle left his parish duties to devote his life to helping to heal the lives of gang members and ex-offenders.

He founded Homeboy Industries, the largest gang rehabilitation and reentry program in the world. For over 30 years, it has provided training and support for formerly gang-involved and previously incarcerated people, allowing them to redirect their lives and become contributing members of society.

## We Are in a Global Transformation

These are just a few of the organizations that are already changing the world by helping us to include love, kindness, service and compassion into our daily lives. They are just the tip of the iceberg of transformation that is happening on our planet, often unnoticed and under reported.

We are in a time of world-wide transition, and we all have the opportunity to be a part of the birth of the new world we wish to see. What part would you like to play?

We're grateful that you are on this journey with us.

With love from our hearts to yours,

*Pat and Larry*

## A Grateful Day

*Gratitude begins in our hearts, then dovetails into behavior.*
*It almost always makes you want to be of service,*
*which is where the joy resides.*

Anne Lamott

How often do you stop to think about all that you feel grateful for?

It's easy to get so caught up in what is happening in the world around us that we allow feelings of anger or fear or overwhelm to poison our daily lives.

A simple fix is to shift to gratitude. We can look around and notice all that we may be taking for granted – then the magic happens. We return to joy.

Then, from a place of gratitude and joy, we find it easy to spread kindness wherever we go.

We're grateful that you are on this journey with us.

With love from our hearts to yours,

*Pat and Larry*

# Carry On

*A hero is an ordinary individual who finds the strength to persevere*
*and endure in spite of overwhelming obstacles.*

Christopher Reeve

In considering the factors that support us on our kindness journey, I realized that friends play a key role. When we have someone we can talk to about anything - knowing they will listen, support us, challenge us when we need it – that provides a container in which we get to know ourselves and each other.

Friendship is a special expression of love, and it can support us as we go out in the world with the intention of bringing kindness with us wherever we go.

All friendships are a gift. Some are comfortable. Some are challenging. Some help us to grow in unexpected ways.

This week, I was introduced to a video that celebrates an extraordinary friendship between two young men with severe disabilities who defied all expectations in rising above their physical challenges – together.

Dartanyon Crockett and Leroy Sutton demonstrate the power of friendship and the triumph of the human spirit over extreme obstacles. It blew my heart wide open.

We're grateful that you are on this journey with us.

With love from our hearts to yours,

*Pat and Larry*

## Tapping into the Power of Your Heart

*It is the heart always that sees, before the head can see.*
… Thomas Carlyle

The heart is the seat of our power. It holds wisdom that the head cannot reach. It's in our hearts where we remember that we are connected and that we belong to each other.

Everything starts here. What we hold in our hearts shows up in our lives – not just in what we give out, but also in what comes back to us.

When we live from our hearts, we become a channel for love to flow out into the world with its transforming power. We remember that we are all one family.

We are all energy beings, and whatever feelings we hold within us determine the energy that radiates out to those around us. By choosing love, we are not just choosing a wonderful feeling. We are choosing to show up as the highest expression of who we are.

This enables us to relate to others without judgment or disapproval. We are open, receptive, and able to respond with compassion and patience. Others feel the loving energy and they respond to it, as well as to our words and actions.

This sounds simple, but we often find ourselves slipping back to our everyday mind and reacting with annoyance or even just frustration over the physical and emotional demands of our lives. This is understandable.

Be patient with yourself. Take it one step at a time.

We can choose to bring love into any situation. We can step back, take a deep breath, and respond with kindness, no matter how the other person is acting. It takes practice, but over time, it becomes easier.

It is all about how we want to be in the world. Do we want to be in charge of how we show up in the world? By reacting to others in the way they act toward us, we are giving away our power.

It is easy to get pulled off the kindness path but tapping back into your heart will return you to your center of power.

The heart is also the center of our intuition. No matter what we are facing in our daily lives, when we receive a feeling or a thought to take a certain action that we have not been thinking about, that is a message from our deeper knowing that there is a better way to proceed than what our mind is telling us.

I have had many experiences that demonstrate the power of intuition in my life. One occurred when I was a single mom. We needed to move, since the house we were renting had been sold. I went out every evening after work to look in neighborhoods I liked to find a house with a For Rent sign. One evening I was headed for an area I liked. While stopped for a red light, I had an urge to turn left, so I let go of my original intention and followed that urging. I drove one block and had another urge to turn left.

A few houses up that street was a house with a For Rent sign. I wrote down the phone number to call – this was long before cell phones – and I drove home and called the number. I got an appointment to meet her at the house the following evening.

When I arrived at the house, I met the woman I had spoken with, but there was also a couple looking at the house as well. We toured the house, and it was perfect for us, with an enclosed yard for our dog.

I held my breath as the couple explained that it was also perfect for them. The woman said that since I had called 5 minutes earlier than they had, I could have the house. My long search was over.

Intuition. It is within us, but where does it come from? I believe it comes from a source of knowing that is beyond us, yet still within us. It's part of the mystery of life. I don't need to understand it. I have simply learned to trust it.

So living from our heart serves us in so many ways. It enables us to be in this world guided by our deeper wisdom and powered by love.

What more can we ask?

We're grateful that you are on this journey with us.

With love from our hearts to yours,

*Pat and Larry*

## Always Stay Humble and Kind

*Humility is not thinking less of yourself,*
*it is thinking of yourself less.*
C. S. Lewis

Staying humble and kind seems like a prerequisite for being in service to others. This means that our journey on our kindness path is directed by our heart - not from a desire of the ego to be recognized and appreciated, but from a true sense of kinship with one another - from love that naturally wells up in us.

We recently received an email from Orly Wahba of Life Vest Inside. Orly is dedicating her life to spreading messages that support us in living with kindness. In this message, she shared her perspective on humility.

Orly suggested that we think about a 1,000-piece puzzle, with pieces of different shapes and colors, but each the same size. That represents humanity. We are each unique. We all have a place in the big picture, and without each contribution, the picture would be incomplete. Seeing this enables us to embrace each person for who they are and not judge them for showing up in the way they do.

We may not understand how certain pieces fit in, but that is because the puzzle is still growing, and we can't see the final picture. Orly suggests that "Our job is to respect each piece for what it adds to the final picture."

That image makes it easier for us to see the value and the beauty of each person we meet, and to see ourselves as equally important in the larger picture of humanity. For me, that is humbling, but also empowering. It reminds me that my piece matters as much as anyone else's, so my only job is to live each day as the best me I can be.

We're grateful that you are on this journey with us.

With love from our hearts to yours,

*Pat and Larry*

## Gratitude is the Wellspring of Kindness

*The Root of joy is gratefulness. It is not joy that makes us grateful.*
*it is gratitude that makes us joyful.*
Brother David Steindl-Rast

What do we do when we hear about everything that is going wrong in the world? It is so easy to let our minds carry us into visions of a future that we cannot control – that will threaten all the good we have in our lives.

At times like that, how do we get back to feeling good about our lives?

For me, the quickest way to shift my energy is to think about the things in my life that I feel good about:

- The people I love and who love me
- Special times with my husband when we share what is in our hearts and minds
- The kindnesses I have received or observed others receiving
- The things in my life that I appreciate – the beauty of the world around me, my home, and the items that make my daily life easier and more pleasant
- Things that give me joy
- Thoughts of my daughter, my son, and my granddaughters

I think about my granddaughter, Mia, who, after lunch in a restaurant with her mom, shared her take-home bag with a homeless man they met on the street. I think of the acts of kindness I have received and observed - reminding me of the good in the people around me.

As I consider gratitude, I realize that it provides an energy within me that makes it easier for me to be kind. Being grateful fills me with a feeling of appreciation that colors everything I see, every person I encounter.

The key is to catch ourselves as our thoughts take us deeper into fear or anger or despair – then shift to thoughts of gratitude.

We benefit immediately, because those thoughts feel good – and the energy we send out to the world around us will uplift and embrace others. From those feelings, we are naturally inclined to kindness.

Some of my inspiration comes from Brother David Steindl-Rast, of Gratefulness.org. He reminds us that "Everything is a gift. If we were aware of this, gratefulness would overwhelm us. But we go through life in a daze."

So, how do we become more grateful? "By becoming aware that every moment is a gift."

"This moment," he says, "with all the opportunities it contains is the most valuable thing ever given to us. If we miss the opportunity of this moment, then another moment is given to us and another moment."

That got me thinking about how I am using the moments in my day? How can I live with more gratitude?

Brother David has a simple practice he calls, "Stop. Look. Go."

### Stop.

Wherever you are, remember to stop what you're doing for a moment. Get quiet.

### Look.

Open your eyes and all your senses for the wonderful richness that is around you at this moment. Open your heart to the opportunity before you.

### Go

When we open our hearts to what lies before us in that moment, life usually offers us the opportunity to enjoy the beauty or inspiration before us. Sometimes it is an opportunity to help others, which requires something from us. We can see it as a gift of the moment – an invitation from life for us to act with kindness.

At this moment, I am feeling deep gratitude for a 4-week long experience I recently shared with 70 people from around the world. We shared our stories, read uplifting articles, answered questions that invited us to go deep and discover more about ourselves and to share what we learned. Strangers became family. Hesitance turned into eager sharing. Creative ideas blossomed, and commitments were made to live a life of service.

We were members of a "Laddership Pod," one of several programs offered by ServiceSpace - an organization run entirely by volunteers. ServiceSpace leverages technology to encourage everyday people around the world to do small acts of service. Our aim is to ignite the fundamental generosity in ourselves and others, creating both inner and outer transformation.

I am still filled with gratitude for the expanding, life enriching experience of sharing that journey with so many kind, generous people with open hearts and minds.

Gratefulness can change our world in immensely important ways. Perhaps the most important is that it lays the foundation from which we are inclined to take our love out into the world through acts of kindness and generosity, feeling our kinship with one another.

And with our gratitude and kindness, we bring joy to ourselves and everyone we meet.

We're grateful that you are on this journey with us.

With love from our hearts to yours,

*Pat and Larry*

## Living with Awe and Wonder

*Wisdom begins in wonder*
~ Socrates

What do awe and wonder have to do with kindness? All my life, I have treasured memories of a few, dramatic moments when I felt awe and wonder, but I never connected those experiences to my interactions with other people. Recently, I read an article by Dacher Keltner that broadened my appreciation of the role that those experiences can play in our lives.

Keltner is a professor of psychology at The University of California, Berkeley, where he directs the Berkeley Social Interaction Lab. Studies conducted by the lab showed that participants experiencing awe seemed to be more inclined to help someone in need afterwards. They also reported feeling less entitled and self-important than the other study participants who had not experienced awe.

Awe contributes to feelings of connection with others, which leads to acts of kindness. Who knew?

So how do we get more awe in our lives?

When I think of awe and wonder, my first thoughts go to large, dramatic scenes of Nature – a star-lit night away from city lights, a waterfall, the view from a mountain top. Stopping to take in the beauty and magnificence before us takes us out of our busy, daily mind and transports us into an altered state.

Now that we can see so much more than ever before, thanks to telescopes that peer deep into the universe, we are treated to awe-inspiring shows of beauty from light years away. These also give us some perspective on our place in the universe.

### The Pale Blue Dot

An image taken, at Carl Sagan's suggestion, by Voyager 1 on 14 February 1990. As Sagan describes it, "Voyager 1 was about 6.4 billion kilometers (4 billion miles) away when it captured this portrait of our world. Caught in the center of scattered light rays (a result of taking the picture so close to the Sun)."

Sagan reflected, "There is perhaps no better demonstration of the folly of human conceits than this distant image of our tiny world. To me, it underscores our responsibility to deal more kindly with one another, and to preserve and cherish the pale blue dot, the only home we've ever known."

For many of us, seeing how small our world is in relation to the universe in which it exists does not disempower us, but instills in us a sense of commitment to our home planet and to one another. Kindness can arise from awe.

### Every Day Wonder

Wonder also arises from the small, ordinary things that we encounter every day, but often do not notice. When we stop to look at the details of our world, we see beauty right in front of us – so many reasons to be amazed at the miracles around us.

When my daughter, Christie, was a toddler, we went for walks up our street. She often stopped to look closely at details that I hardly noticed. I still have a picture in my mind of her expression of sheer delight as she looked at a flower blooming at the side of the road. She turned to me with a look of wonder and pointed to the flower. I hadn't looked closely at it as I passed it on my early morning walks. As I took in the details – the colors and shapes – I felt gratitude for such loveliness in my world, and I realized that I had not taken the time to stop and appreciate the beauty around me every day.

So many things in our lives inspire feelings of awe – lightning and thunder, the play of sun and shadow on a mountainside, a spider weaving her web, dew drops all over the garden, lady bugs, turtles, rabbits, bird songs, butterflies, different colored rocks in a stream bed, blossoming trees in the spring and falling leaves in autumn. The list is endless.

We can get so busy or distracted that we fail to notice, but we do live in an awesome world. Let's stop more often and look at the wonders before us and let love and appreciation well up within us. Then, let's take those feelings with us as we go through our day, and surely, we will be inclined to meet others with appreciation and kindness.

We're grateful that you are on this journey with us.

With love from our hearts to yours,

*Pat and Larry*

# A Time to Remember Our Kinship

*We are here to awaken*
*from our illusion of separateness.*
... Thich Nhat Hanh

Religious ceremonies have been used for millennia to bring people together, to create a sense of community, of belonging. Unfortunately, that sense of belonging has also been used to create a sense of difference from others who follow other spiritual paths. The very experience of oneness that we feel when together in a familiar setting of a church, synagogue, mosque, temple – feeling the presence of a higher, loving power that protects us and guides our lives – the same experience has also been used to separate us from others who follow a different tradition.

We are at a time in history that requires us to put those ideas of separation aside and remember our kinship with one another – not just those who are like us, but with all others sharing the Earth with us.

All religions teach us to love one another. So, how did we get it so wrong through history and use our differences to hate and fear one another?

In our religious traditions, we all have ways of greeting one another with love and respect.

Shalom (peace), Salaam (peace), Peace be with you, Namaste (I bow to you). These greetings carry a message of respect and honor that says, "I wish you well."

I was pleased to see the spirit of these ancient greetings show up in our modern culture. In the science fiction movie, Avatar, the indigenous people on a planet that had been invaded had a simple greeting for one another – "I see you." That says so much in so few words.

That rephrases all the religious greetings in a way that speaks to us today.

Do we really see each other - not just superficially, but in a deeper way, recognizing our inter-connection, our kinship? As we encounter each other in our daily lives, do we see the differences that separate us, that trigger judgments that cause us to turn away rather than reach out?

How different our response could be if we silently said, "I see you" to every person we meet, and we saw the deeper truth – this is another myself – he or she has had their own life journey different from mine, but we each came into this life from the same loving Source, and we are each doing the best we know how to do in this moment.

Have you ever been judged for something you said or something you did or for how you looked? Was there something inside of you calling out to be seen for all of who you are, not just the way you are showing up in this moment?

The way we see each other – those we know and those we are just meeting – affects the way we respond to them. When we decide to live with kindness, it's useful to have mental tools that help us stay in our hearts and not let our ego jump in with all of its judgments.

"I see you" puts us back in our hearts – it is calling on us to see beyond the way someone is expressing in this moment and see the deeper truth of our essential kinship.

Can we do this?

We all have the power of choice. As we choose this as a silent mantra when we're out in the world, we will see no stranger, just family we have yet to meet.

You may find that this is a way to expand your kindness journey - to open new opportunities for you to take your love out into the world.

As you read these words, no matter where you are, please know that I see you, and I appreciate your being in my life.

We're grateful that you are on this journey with us.
With love from our hearts to yours,
*Pat and Larry*

## Kindness as Currency in the Gifting Economy

*For it is in giving that we receive.*
~ Saint Francis of Assisi

This week, I want to take you down a more personal path, to show you the power of kindness in an individual life. What we give in this world does return to us in a way that meets our needs at the perfect time. This story also demonstrates the powerful economy of gifting, in which the currency is kindness, rather than money.

This is Bill's story.

We met Bill at the Haywood Street Church, where we volunteered to be in community with our unhoused neighbors. He had spent the previous two years trying to prevent the progression of renal disease in his body. Circumstances in his life brought him to Asheville at the time that his kidneys had failed, and he needed to begin dialysis. When we met him, Larry and I both had an inner recognition that he is part of our family.

With his savings depleted and unable to work to earn a living, he was about to be homeless. We invited him into our home and our lives, a decision that enriched our lives in many ways. Bill is a kind, generous person who enjoys being of service to others. He was a welcome member of our family, joyfully contributing to household chores.

The three of us also continued to be part of the Haywood Street Community, being part of a weekly Story Circle, in which people came together to tell their stories and share ideas about life. We also joined others at the Welcome Table and enjoyed a home cooked meal with our neighbors who live on the street, including them in our lives.

Living on disability income, Bill had few options, but three years ago, he was able to get a nice apartment in a building subsidized by the federal government. He immediately made friends with many of the elderly residents, and he became the go-to person for anyone who needed help with electronics or fixing whatever broke.

Then came the big surprise that made him wonder how he deserved it. A life-long friend gave him the car he had bought for his daughter when she went to college. He bought her a new one when she graduated, and he gave the old one to Bill. Now Bill was able to help his friends even more, taking them grocery shopping or taking their shopping lists with him when he went to the store.

A year ago, on Christmas day, he got a call that a kidney had become available for him, and the next day, he got the best Christmas gift he had ever received. After a short recovery from the transplant surgery, he began his new life, free of dialysis.

One of his favorite people is 100-year-old Myrtle. Last October, she fell and called Bill. He called for an ambulance and followed her to the hospital. For the next few days, he visited her and took care of things back home. Then, for the next few months, he spent time with her daily, helping her with whatever she needed, including helping her granddaughter plan her 100th birthday party.

Myrtle is doing well now. Bill still takes her shopping and runs errands for her, and always answers the phone when she calls, even in the middle of the night. He is there for her.

Meanwhile, he continues to take care of other friends, including Tyler, who sometimes needs help shopping. He has been a good friend to her, encouraging her through some difficult times. They have also become closer, and he has been spending more time with her.

Recently, Bill's car developed a serious issue that required a repair more expensive than the car was worth. Tyler said he could use her car to do her shopping, and she recently told Bill that, not only can he use her car whenever he needs it, but she has added a codicil to her will, leaving her car to him.

It is hard to take in the immensity of what seem to be unearned gifts, but Bill's life demonstrates the power of kindness and the sure but mysterious way that what we give returns to us. He is constantly giving to others without expecting anything back, and now, what he needs comes into his life.

His experience is an example of the gifting economy, which is a very healthy sub-set of our financial economy. The currency of the gifting economy is not money, but gifts that we give to others – not in exchange for something back, but as natural expressions of our innate kindness. These include our time and attention, our knowledge and skills, our love and compassion.

We have a vibrant gifting economy in our country and around the world – people helping friends in unexpected ways, looking out for one another, volunteering at local charities or hospitals or schools.

Bill has given freely and abundantly, so, of course, it has to flow back to him in the form of what he needs. It is difficult for most of us to see his new way of life as an alternative form of economy, but it has been with us for millennia at the personal level, and it was a way of life in indigenous cultures around the world.

As the world changes, we will still be able to live with kindness, to share our gifts with one another and to receive back what we need. This is an economy made possible by community, an expression of remembering that we belong to one another.

If you are reading this, you are already living with kindness. Please share with us ways that you are participating in the gifting economy.

We're grateful that you are on this journey with us.
With love from our hearts to yours,
*Pat and Larry*

# Kindness as the Heart of a Local Economy

*The measure of your life will not be in
what you accumulate, but what you give away.*
~ Dr. Wayne Dyer

In my last post, I shared the story of our friend, Bill, whose recent life experience exemplifies the gift economy, which is a very healthy sub-set of our financial economy. The currency of the gifting economy is not money, but gifts that we give to others – not in exchange for something back, but as natural expressions of our innate kindness. These include our time and attention, our knowledge and skills, our love and compassion.

We have a vibrant gifting economy in our country and around the world – people helping friends in unexpected ways, sharing what they have, looking out for one another, volunteering at local charities or hospitals or schools.

As Bill's experience shows us, as we give to others as an expression of kindness, not looking for something in return, what we need does flow to us as well.

Our financial system operates on the principle that every interaction is a transaction – I give what I have – money, goods or skill – in exchange for what you give me. The gift economy uses another layer of currency that is given without a calculated exchange.

People are kind and generous by nature. Just watch very young children. They often enjoy sharing what they have and receiving a smile and words of appreciation from others.

This is our nature. Unfortunately, it can easily be suppressed by the idea that we have to earn everything we receive and that others must give us something back every time we share. I am not advocating an economy without money. But I am suggesting that we can expand our participation in the growing gift economy in which we share what we have and receive from others what they give freely.

There are many examples of vibrant gift economies in the world today. A good example is The Buy Nothing Project.

On a trip to Nepal, Liesl Clark and her family witnessed how the Nepalese cared for each other, insisting on sharing gifts equally within the community and taking responsibility for the aging, fragile, and infirm. She returned home, eager to see if these principles could be applied to their area and possibly beyond.

Liesl and her friend Rebecca Rockefeller began The Buy Nothing Project with a Facebook page and a list of ideals. Their intention was "to focus more on community and connections and less on stuff, thereby removing physical wealth from the equation. The project encourages the feeling that we are all connected and that everyone has something to offer."

We all have something to give –

- items we don't use or excess produce from the garden
- time to sit with someone or help someone move or clean out their garage
- information to help others solve a problem
- skills to share, such as music, or to create something for others – cooking, sewing, fixing what is broken

The list is endless.

We're grateful that you are on this journey with us.

With love from our hearts to yours,

*Pat and Larry*

## What Does Kindness Have to Do with Activism?

*So that lesson from the river was that when*
*we operate from a deep love, then we're unstoppable.*
Mark Dubois

We believe that kindness is love with its work boots on. It means taking our love out into the world and making a difference - in the lives of the people we meet in our daily life or sometimes, in our community or in the world.

As I considered the different ways in which we act in the world, I thought about activism, which is a dramatic form of action. So, I turned to my trusty resource, dictionary.com, and this is what it said about activism:

"the doctrine or practice of vigorous action or involvement as a means of achieving political or other goals, sometimes by demonstrations, protests, etc."

In our culture today, we see activism as cultural and political protest, but it is much more. It can take the form of determined advocacy at various levels of government. It can take the form of written or video advocacy to inform the public of an important issue. In some cases, it can be a dramatic single act to bring attention to a current or impending tragedy. The causes behind activism often relate to human rights issues, but sometimes they spring from our love for an individual, a group of people or for nature.

Often acts of activism seem to fail, but with persistence, over time, as more people are inspired to get involved, they bring results – an awakening in our culture to the importance of an issue that had not been generally recognized before. In the United States, the civil rights movement in the 1960s and the racial justice movement today are good examples of the power of activism.

I want to focus on a different kind of activism – acts of courage and commitment by an individual to take a stand against great odds to protect something of value or to make a powerful statement in a time of crisis. Sometimes, individual acts courage stand-out from the background of a larger demonstration.

On June 5, 1989, the world watched as pro-democracy student protestors were forcibly cleared from Beijing's Tiananmen Square. As a line of tanks entered the square to disband the protestors, one man stood in front of the first tank and caused them to stop. Very quickly, other protestors pulled him away. He did not stop the massacre, but his dramatic act of courage inspired people world-wide.

In Baton Rouge, Louisiana, on 9 July 2016, 28-year-old Ieshia Evans was part of a peaceful demonstration against the shooting by police of Alton Sterling. As two cops in riot gear approached her, she showed dignity and determination, taking a stand for a safer future for her son. Her graceful act of resistance personified peaceful protest in stark contrast to the violence of the police response.

These examples came from the context of an existing demonstration and drew additional attention to the cause. Sometimes, an individual's act of courage and commitment inspire others to join in a cause that had not gotten much attention.

Mark Dubois grew up in the Sierra Nevada Mountains in California. He had a passionate love for the Stanislaus River Canyon, a beautiful pristine river valley with limestone caves, sliding rocks, deep pools of water and vigorous rapids where water enthusiasts could go kayaking and rafting downstream. He was a river guide, and he spent every hour he could in the place he loved.

Then, in 1973, the U.S. Army Corps of Engineers prepared to open a new dam project, flooding miles of the Canyon. Mark and a few river advocates did everything they could to convince politicians and the public that the price was too high – to lose such a natural treasure.

Their efforts failed, and with no other way to stop the destruction of the canyon, Mark chained himself to a boulder behind the New Melones Dam and threw away the key. "If you guys are going to flood 9 million years of evolution, why not take one more creature with you," he said.

His willingness to give his life to protect the place he loved got national attention. Eventually, the governor's office agreed to monitor the water level, and Mark ended his protest. Unfortunately, with deeper water, the character of the river was dramatically changed, and the free-flowing stream was turned into a dead zone above the reservoir.

Mark's passionate fight for the life of the river he loved focused national attention on the destruction of irreplaceable natural resources caused by the building of dams at a time when other sources of power were available. Many outdoor enthusiasts were inspired to become river activists and to work to protect the rivers in California. With more public awareness, politicians were persuaded to oppose other proposed dams. In the next six years, Mark and the river activists saved four other rivers from similar destruction.

People are willing to commit their time and passion to promote or protect something they love. "Once our heart is open," Mark said, "then the other attributes of conscious activism come into play. But the first step is falling in love. The rest flows from there."

In looking at the examples above, it is clear that Mark loved the river on which he spent so much of his early life. What love inspired others to their actions?

The protestors in Beijing were fighting for more political freedom, and their love was for the vision of a more open and free society. For the protestors in Baton Rouge, the love for their families and their own desire for a safer, more just society fueled their passionate opposition to a police culture that allowed unjustified killing of Black men.

In the process of researching and writing this, I gained a deeper understanding of activism. Now, whenever I see or read about demonstrations for or against something, I will ask myself, "What do they love?" What quality of life do they want more of or what are they fighting against that prevents them from having a missing quality in their lives – or in someone else's life?

In looking at life through a lens of kindness, I will now consider how love or lack of love impacts any situation that I am viewing. It is also helpful to consider how love or lack of it impacts my own response to it.

The further I go on this kindness path, the more it asks of me, and the more likely I am to step off the path. It is so easy to fall back to old ways of judgment of others and out of the love that wants to understand them.

The kindness path does not demand perfection. It gently calls us back when we have stepped off.

We're grateful that you are on this journey with us.

With love from our hearts to yours,

*Pat and Larry*

## Joy and Delight in an Uncertain World

*Joy is what happens to us when we allow ourselves
to recognize how good things really are."*

Marianne Williamson

Several writings about joy and delight came to me in the past few days. Each offered a different perspective on the unlimited opportunities for joy all around us wherever we are. It became clear that this was meant to be our theme for the week.

In *3 Easy Ways to Bring More Gratitude into Your Life*, Nick Polizzi suggests that creating a daily gratitude habit will bring more joy, health and abundance into your life. He offers three simple, daily exercises:

1. Each morning, say a simple "thank you" for another new day of life.
2. Choose a meal each day to reflect on a few things that you're grateful for in that moment.
3. Write down one thing you are grateful for every day for the next ten days.

Perhaps you will enjoy it so much that it will become a habit.

Nick offers some suggestions to help get you started:

- What you like about yourself, inside and out.
- Can you derive some bit of wisdom from a challenge you are currently facing?
- List your favorite people and what you love about them.
- Perhaps take a moment to focus on the good parts of your job, the work you get to do, the people you get to do it with, and the compensation you receive for it.
- What are the things you love about where you live?
- What is your favorite color? How does it make you feel?
- Have you received any kind words or praise lately?
- What are you good at? Do you have hidden talents?
- What are you looking forward to in life?
- Was the sky particularly beautiful today?

How can you be more open to the gifts that life is bringing to you today?

Often, little things can bring as much joy as those that are bigger and more obvious. We simply need to notice them and spend a few moments in appreciation.

In *Six Notes on Tenderness,* Kerri Rosenstein shares six memories from her life that she remembers as tender moments, inviting us to be aware of the gift that such moments offer us as we go through our daily lives.

Her mother peeling an orange for her and leaving it on her bed while she studied for an exam. Fresh fruit as a gift of love.

A handwritten note on her pillow, telling her that his grandma's grateful she is in her grandson's life. A gentle welcome into a family.

As children, she and her brother are in their bathing suits at the pool. When it starts raining, she says, "Dear, God, please, let it stop raining so we can swim." Her father gently says, "Did you know there's a farmer somewhere who's been praying for rain? This is the answer to his prayer." Wisdom coming in unexpected ways.

Gathering pine cones with her grandmother to build a bonfire for the rest of her grandchildren and great-nieces and nephews. As her grandmother is inside preparing the food, she hears them all laughing together, and she smiles warmly, seeing her descendants joyful, when she had overcome so much in her life to bring them to this moment.

Less than one week after she met her boyfriend, they went to drop off her cousin at the airport. He witnessed a tender moment when she hugged her cousin goodbye with teary eyes. After that, they sat and talked until early morning - almost strangers beginning a long journey together.

Her aunt told her that when her son was born, she'd go to his cradle in the middle of the night and weep, because she'd never loved someone this much in her whole life, and she was not sure how to protect him in a dangerous world. The power of pure love in an uncertain world.

Can you remember tender moments you have had in your life? How do we bring more of those into our lives now?

In *The Book of Delights,* Ross Gay writes about the small joys we often overlook in our busy lives, our shared bonds, and the rewards that come from a life closely observed. Almost every day for a year, he looked for and wrote about moments of delight, and he encourages us to create space in our lives to experience delight.

In a conversation with Krista Tippett, *Tending Joy and Practicing Delight,* Ross talks about the experience of writing the book and what he discovered from a year of looking for delight every day.

He sees joy as a calling, precisely in a moment like this. "If you and I know we're each in the process (of dying), there is something that will happen between us. There's some kind of tenderness that might be possible." He talks about the delight of tenderness as ordinary, transformative experiences.

In writing the Delights book, he was asking the question, "What is this joy?" or "How joy?" For him, that is a life question. He came to see that joy is the moments when his alienation – from people and from all that he was dealing with – goes away.

"If it was a visual thing, everything becomes luminous. And I love that mycelium, forest metaphor, that there's this thing connecting us. And among the things of that thing connecting us is that we have this common experience — many common experiences, but a really foundational one is that we are not here forever."

Ross describes it as a joining – a "joy-ning." "It is joy by which the labor that will make the life that I want, possible. It is not at all puzzling to me that joy is possible in the midst of difficulty."

In discussing advocacy, he said, "I often think the gap in our speaking about and for justice, or working for justice, is that we forget to advocate for what we love, for what we find beautiful and necessary." When we experience delight, he observed, we want to share it with others.

What is giving you delight, today? Think of something small or large.

What comes to mind?

This focus may shift your day to one of joy.

We're grateful that you are on this journey with us.

With love from our hearts to yours,

*Pat and Larry*

# When Does Kindness Require Us to Act?

*The opposite for courage is not cowardice,*
*it is conformity. Even a dead fish can go with the flow.*
Jim Hightower

Living with kindness is a way of being in the world that is rewarding and uplifts our spirits. As we offer a smile and kind words, others respond favorably. When we reach out to help someone in need, everyone involved is uplifted by the encounter.

But sometimes we find ourselves in a situation that is asking us to step out of our comfort zone. It may require us to speak out or take action when others around us are not willing to do so. Something inside of us knows that our response could make a difference, but we are reluctant to help.

This is called "the bystander effect." When the situation calls for action, but no one else is helping, it is easier to be influenced by group thinking. We can tell ourselves, "It is none of my business" or "Someone else could help, why should it be me?"

This is a common occurrence, and it was dramatically demonstrated in a video I watched this week.

### The Bystander Effect

In the video, actors present different scenarios to test the responses from the public. We are not surprised when a seemingly drunk man lying on the sidewalk gets ignored. No one stops or even seems to notice him. Later, when a scruffy-looking man lying on his side and clearly in pain calls out for someone to help him, people simply ignore him, as well.

In another scenario in the same location, a well-dressed man sits down on the sidewalk with his head in his hands, and almost immediately, someone stops and asks him if he is okay. Then others gather around him, with a group response of kindness.

I was surprised to see that when a respectably dressed woman is seemingly unconscious, for several minutes, people just walk past her. Finally, someone stops to help, and another woman, who had walked past her and looked back, also joined in. It seems that some people need someone else to indicate the proper response before they will help.

We seem to live by two contradictory rules: We ought to help someone in need and we ought to do what everyone else is doing. With the crowd mentality, we allow a group of strangers to set the precedent not to help someone in need. When several other people have noticed and done nothing, we are more likely to do nothing as well.

If one person responds in a caring way, however, others often join in. It takes just one person who has the courage to break from the crowd, deciding to do the right thing, whether others show up or not. When we find ourselves in a situation like this, we are challenged to expand our kindness practice.

In another video, we see other examples:

## The Bystander Effect - Why Some People Act and Others Don't

Kelly Charles-Collins talks about situations in which people are afraid to intervene, because it may put them in danger. In that case, calling others to help might bring a collective response. If there is no way to intervene, recording the incident on your phone could be helpful later. But if someone else is in danger, Kelly says, just ignoring it or becoming a passive bystander is not just lack of action. It is indifference.

She tells a true story from her own life. Her son Jordan had just finished eating in a restaurant when he was approached by cops and violently handcuffed and arrested. Out of a crowd of witnesses, one woman stood up for him, repeating over and over that he had done nothing wrong – at risk to herself. In the investigation that followed and in the court hearing, her testimony changed the outcome in his favor.

Kelly also talked about the bystander effect in social media, which allows us to interact, but also enables us to bully others. She shared research that shows that between 10 and 40 percent of adolescents are victims of cyber bullying, and 70% of adults have witnessed some form of online harassment. Most people simply receive those posts, but even when they are uncomfortable, say nothing..

She gave an example of a woman who witnessed a girl being raped, and instead of trying to help, she took a video of it and later, posted it on social media. Her video was liked and shared. It became entertainment. Kelly asks a question we all need to consider. "When did we become numb to all of this?"

**This is an opportunity for kindness to step up.**

Crime and cyber bullying have become entertainment, and we seem to have lost our empathy for people being victimized. The group mentality of people who don't even know each other lends itself to the bystander effect. We can always choose not to go along. We can speak up and give voice to our disgust at what we are seeing. Others may need to see someone else object in order for them to have the courage to take a stand as well.

When we find ourselves in one of these situations, we want to be kind, but we're not sure what the consequences will be if we do. How do we have the courage to go from being a bystander to being an active witness?

I have come to believe that there is a reason for whatever shows up in my life. With that realization, these situations seem like an opportunity to expand my comfort zone, and I am more likely to step up and take whatever action seems to be needed.

I remember that kindness is love in action. I ask myself,

"What would Love do?" "What would I want someone else to do if that were me or someone that I love needing help?"

A kind intervention can bring a positive outcome to a painful situation. It uplifts us, the person we help, and anyone who witnesses our act of kindness. When people have witnessed someone else's kindness, they are more likely to intervene the next time they are called upon to help another person. There can be a ripple effect from one act of courage.

We are all learning as we continue our kindness journeys. Sometimes, we make choices that we later wish we had not. That's part of the journey, and each experience helps us to decide how we want to take the next step.

When we do have the courage to take kind action, we become stronger, and those around us see a possibility for their own lives.

I wish you peace, love and courage on your journey.

We're grateful that you are on this journey with us.

With love from our hearts to yours,

*Pat and Larry*

## The Power of Small Acts of Kindness

*Not all of us can do great things,*
*but we can do small things with great love.*
… Mother Teresa

Kindness is the way we spread love in the world. It feels good - in the giving and receiving. The more we experience kindness, the more we connect with others and reinforce the awareness of our kinship. That is how the world changes - when we remember our kinship.

The photo above speaks for all of us. The photographer, Matt Collamer of Unsplash, said that he met Michael in a Boston subway station and told him that he liked his sign. "What matters is what it means to you," Michael said. When asked what it meant to him, Michael replied, "Doing a deed or expressing kindness to another person without expecting anything in return."

Matt said he loves approaching strangers wherever he goes. "Listening and talking to them teaches you about people and how similar we all are to one another. Just like Michael, we're all seeking human kindness."

We agree. Wanting more of the pleasure we receive from our connection with others, Larry and I have looked for new opportunities to be kind. Some were right in front of us, and we hadn't noticed. We want to share with you our expanded appreciation of small acts of kindness.

You are already living your life with kindness, and we know that you have ideas to share with us, as well. Here are some that now guide our lives.

### Look for ways to say thank you.

It is easy to say, "Thank you," in response to every thoughtful action, no matter how small it may be. "Thank you" acknowledges the other person's kindness. We can take that brief connection to a deeper level by adding a comment that expresses our appreciation for their kindness. "You're very kind" or "I appreciate your kindness" gets a warm response. Once in a while, we share our favorite definition of kindness, "love with its work boots on," as a way of acknowledging their kindness to us.

Larry has taken this practice to another level. In the grocery store he looks for the woman who arranges the flower display to thank her for the pleasure it gives him to walk by. He notices the man stocking the shelves and stops to say it looks good. Of course, a thank you to the cashier is easy. An additional comment about how busy she is let's her know someone noticed. Once in a while, he mentions to the store manager how good it is to shop where everyone is pleasant and helpful.

Standing in the checkout line offers an opportunity to connect with people. Larry often uses humor to begin a conversation. Seeing a basket full of wine, beer and snacks, he might ask, "Having a party?" If he gets a positive response, he may say, "What was that address again?"

Most people respond well to a little humor, and it leads to a conversation, no matter how brief.

Learning how to ask for help is an important part of our journey – giving other people the opportunity to be kind. Larry has difficulty bending over enough to reach the ground, so when he drops his keys or something else, he looks for someone to ask for help. "Would you do me a favor?" always gets a positive response. That gives him a chance to say, "I'm Larry. I appreciate your kindness."

### Look for ways to be kind online.

Most of my activities are online, and my interactions are with people I don't know and will never meet. But we have a connection, no matter how remote it may be. I recently had an email dialogue with a support person who helped me with a problem. Once it was resolved, he sent me an email with the answer. I wrote him back to thank him for his help and wish him well. To my surprise, he responded to me with a thank you and wished me well.

I then realized that people who work online are less likely to receive thanks for what they do. I have begun to look for ways to respond to them with the same kindness that I offer people in front of me. I now often receive emails in response, and I feel the same energetic boost that I get when someone returns a smile.

Of course, some platforms online are designed to help people reach out to each other. They provide the opportunity to ask for or to offer help, and people often respond, providing the information or other help that people need. During the pandemic, we saw offers of free masks, and offers to help anyone who could not get out by buying groceries, running other errands, or just coming by for a visit. At other times, people have often begun a GoFundMe page for someone else, to raise money for a family with a larger need. People are generous when they see they can help someone else.

### Look for ways to help someone

I remember so many times when someone stepped up to help me. When my children were young and my arms were full, people often held a door for me or offered to help me carry groceries to the car. At this point in my life, I walk with a walker or use a wheelchair when I go out, and strangers often hold the door for me or ask if I need help.

It's easy to notice someone with a cane or walker or in a wheelchair. Others in need may not stand out. As we take our kindness practice to the next level, we can be aware of the people around us, and notice if someone may need help. Reaching out may lead to a new connection that enriches both of you.

Even passing someone on the street is an opportunity for a smile and a nod that acknowledges their presence. That brief connection shows them that we see them. I often add a silent greeting, wishing them well. That deepens my feeling of connection and reminds me of our kinship.

## Practice being present with other people

It is easy to be superficially polite, saying kind words without really connecting with the other person. But when we give them our full attention, we truly relate to them, and we are able to connect with them at a deeper level.

Expressing interest in others - listening to them and asking questions that enable us to know them better – opens the door to a more meaningful relationship. One benefit of listening with genuine interest is that it keeps us in the present and prevents our minds from wandering to what we plan to do next.

As Mary Lou Casey said, "What most people really need is a good listening to." I also like what Will Rogers said, in his inimitable way – "Never miss a good chance to shut up." These are good guidelines for building a relationship, and they have been helpful for me. I used to think that telling people about me was the way to build a relationship, but now I know that being curious about the other person is what opens the door to the next step.

We have come to see that every encounter is a gift. By being fully present, we allow ourselves to find that gift –a chance to help someone or to receive help, a new relationship, learning more about ourselves or others, or perhaps gaining wisdom from the other person.

As we hear the stories of others' lives, we discover how much we have in common and, we also learn how much our life paths have been different. In the process, we may find that we are expanding our circle of compassion.

We believe that love is who we are – and love is the true nature of every person we meet. The more we connect with one another with this realization, the more we experience our kinship, and that is what will ultimately transform this world into a flourishing place of love and kindness.

Thank you for reading this to the end.

We're grateful that you are on this journey with us.

With love from our hearts to yours,

*Pat and Larry*

## Kindness is a Path, Not an Event

*Nothing can make our life, or the lives of other people,*
*more beautiful than perpetual kindness*
… Leo Tolstoy

Every morning, as Larry and I enjoy our coffee and tea, we talk about whatever is on our minds and hearts – a dream from the night before, something we read and want to share, where we are on our kindness journey. We often discuss ways to expand our kindness practice.

Earlier this week, I asked Larry to talk about his experience of kindness at this point in his life. His ideas inspired me, and I want to share them with you.

He talked about waking up in the morning, seeing his day filled with kindness – giving and receiving it. Understanding the transformative power of kindness, he expressed a desire "to transform myself and the world by adding more love to the world."

That is an uplifting intention. We feel good when we smile or say a kind word to someone we meet or help a person in need. We talked about how to let more people into our circle of compassion. That means exploring ways to overcome the resistance we sometimes feel to reach out with kindness when we are presented with an opportunity.

### What gets in the way?

Sometimes, we're just focused on what we're doing, so we pass by others without noticing them. We all do that. It's part of our daily life. But when we are conscious of being in the presence of others, it feels good to look at them and smile, as a way of acknowledging them. Often, we get a smile back, and a connection has been made, if only for a moment.

That is the easy kindness, but how do we find ways to overcome the resistance we sometimes feel to reach out with kindness at other times.

Larry talked about times he wished he had responded but failed to bring kindness to a situation. He may have been too busy to stop and offer help, or he lacked the courage to reach out, not knowing how the person would respond. Now, he's trusting his inner guidance and he is more likely to begin a conversation when his gut tells him "It's ok." He's found that sometimes humor is a good way to begin a conversation.

Often, the obstacle to kindness is the judgments we hold. It is harder to be kind when the other person is being rude or unkind, either to us or to others. Sometimes we have judgments because of what we know about them – perhaps their actions in the past or different political views that set up a wall between us before we get to know each other.

We each have our list of the things that make it harder to feel kind. With any thought or feeling, we experience the energy – whether positive or negative – and send that energy out to the world around us. So, holding a negative feeling about someone has an impact on us and on them. Knowing that is an incentive to be more aware of our thoughts and to give people space to show up as they are in that moment, without needing to approve or disapprove.

This is a challenge for most of us. We are exposed to so much of what is going on in the world that we frequently get triggered. With incomplete information, we can make assumptions about someone that causes us to respond with anger, and that sometimes gets out of control.

## A Powerful Challenge for Me

A video went viral last week, showing a man in a pick-up truck trying to hit a homeless man and his cat. The man was quite shaken by the attack and his cat was almost killed. If the driver had known the man – if he knew the man's story – he may not have wanted to harm him and might have reached out to help. This incident demonstrates one price we pay for the disconnection in our society and the underlying anger that erupts, even with no apparent cause.

So, what can we offer in response? Certainly not demonizing the driver of the truck. Just as he did not know the homeless man's story, we do not know his. We don't know the state of his mental health or what beliefs he grew up with or what life experiences contributed to his rage.

I admit that I did not respond with compassion for him. Only time brought me to a larger perspective. Now I see both men as victims of a larger societal dysfunction. By responding to acts of hate and anger by others with our own anger and judgment, we are contributing to the already toxic mix. So how do we rise above it?

I think of the guidance that Larry and I both received years ago, to be in the world but not of the world. This is an opportunity to practice that. It is easy to get pulled into societal thinking, which is full of judgments that divide us. But we see how much harm comes from that. So how do we rise above those judgments?

One way to do that is to wonder about people instead of judging them – being curious to know more about them, and remembering our kinship, even when we don't know each other. Then it is easier to tune back into the transformative power of love and live with kindness and compassion.

We each get to decide how to do this.

Larry summed it up beautifully – kindness is a path, not an event. He suggested that we grow into a 24/7 consciousness of kindness, rather than seeing kindness as situational. That means noticing people he would not normally talk to and looking for a kind way to connect.

For us, the underlying truth is our essential kinship. Remembering that makes the rest easier.

We were first introduced to the concept of the circle of compassion by Father Gregory Boyle, whose life work has been with former gang members. He has a powerful message of kinship and compassion, and this video will give you a brief glimpse into his journey and his heart.

We're grateful that you are on this journey with us.

With love from our hearts to yours,

*Pat and Larry*

## Kindness Comes from Hearing Each Other

*At the end of the day, you need someone who listens*
*to you with no judgment.*

Payal Rohatgi

I have read a lot about the importance of storytelling lately – the power it has to open doors for understanding between people whose life paths have been different. I see great value in learning about someone else's story as a powerful way to overcome the judgments we may have about others.

I also see the darker side of storytelling – the stories we tell in our minds about ourselves and others. Sometimes, those stories get in the way of our ability to actually hear the stories of others, as we simply overlay them with our preconceived notions of who they are.

We all do it to some extent. We can see it more easily in others than in ourselves.

I have a friend who has a negative view of African American people as a group, even though he has met some Black people whom he seems to care about. He is a kind person, and I thought that I could help him to expand his understanding by sharing a video that gave me insights into the challenges Black people often face in our culture.

The members of a church had invited a Black woman to share her story with them, so they could better understand the realities of her life. She calmly told of experiences that led her to feeling unsafe in the world and fearing for the safety of her children. Her story is a part of the fabric of our culture, and it gave me a glimpse into that part of our world that I had not seen before.

My friend's response was quite different – "They're always complaining," he said. He had not heard the truth of her story.

Wow. I was speechless. We had heard the same words, but we had two different stories in our heads that colored what we heard. How we listen to others matters. Are we open to new information that leads us to better understanding or closed to anything that challenges our beliefs about who people are?

Storytelling is only half of the equation. Listening is the other half, and one without the other is an exercise in wishful thinking. Of course, most people who take the time to hear someone else's story do so to expand their understanding, so it is important to keep telling our stories.

This led me to considering the stories we tell ourselves about who we are.

My friend had a view of himself that contributed to the way that he judged others. He had grown up with privileges not available to many people, and, for most of his life, had opportunities to pursue his dreams and create a good life. He saw himself as being honest and responsible and able to take care of himself, without asking other people to provide what he needed.

As most of us do to some extent, he responded to the actions of others by considering what he would do in their situation. Of course, he would never be in their situation, because it is happening in the context of their lives, not his. But we don't stop to consider that. It is easy to jump to what we would do, and that lays the platform from which we judge someone else's actions.

So, that brings me to how I see myself. This is where it gets tricky. At this point in my life, I see myself as being kind and curious about other people, so it is easier to understand them, no matter how they are showing up today. But that's not all of who I am. I have my own judgments and dislikes, even though I would prefer not to.

I admit that I did not respond to my friend with the same kind of acceptance that I wanted him to give to others. I was willing to consider the life journey of other people before judging them, but I did not, in that moment, consider the factors in his life that had led him to hold his beliefs. I could hear the woman's story with compassion, so why couldn't he?

Wow. Time to look at myself.

This journey we are on – the kindness journey – if we take it seriously, we notice that it offers us many opportunities to grow, to become more of who we want to be. For me, living with kindness means having an open heart and being kind to everyone I meet – not just outwardly, but also within me.

If kindness is an expression of love in the world, then it has to begin with love within me. So, for me, that means dropping any judgments about others and seeing them, each on their unique life journey, doing the best they know how to do in this moment.

That applies to everyone. It means dropping any judgments that I may have that someone "should know better." It means accepting people as they show up in this moment, even in their judgments, knowing that we are each on our own life journey and figuring it out as best we can as we go.

When it comes to storytelling, how we show up in the world is the loudest story we tell. That arises from the stories we tell ourselves – about who we are and who other people are.

Let's be as kind as we can in all of those stories and let our lives unfold from there, so we can help to make the world around us a kinder place.

We're grateful that you are on this journey with us.

With love from our hearts to yours,

*Pat and Larry*

# How Can We Disagree in a Kind Way?

*There ain't no good guy, there ain't no bad guy*
*There's only you and me,*
*and we just disagree.*

Jim Krueger

This quote is from a song that was made popular by Dave Mason in the 1970s. The song is about a personal relationship, but the spirit applies to every aspect of our lives.

How do we think of and respond to someone who has different ideas and ways of being in the world than ours?

Most important is the way we see each other. In the current culture, there are so many calls to see people who have different ideas than ours as enemy. It is easy to believe that "I am right, and you are wrong" or even, "I am one of the good guys, and you are not."

The disrespecting each other over differing ideas has become an epidemic in our culture. How do we stand against that?

**Curiosity is an antidote to judgment.**

We see this as a call for curiosity.

Kindness in action invites us to make an effort to hear the other person, to understand why they think the way they do or do what they do.

If you express genuine interest, they will probably respond in a positive way to an inquiry such as, "That's interesting. Please tell me more about why you think that."

This opens the door to understanding. If we sincerely listen with that intention, it diffuses the impulse to argue and defend our point of view. It is important that we truly listen, and not let our mind wander to prepare for a rebuttal. This is not about proving that my ideas are right and yours are wrong. It is a way to build a bridge, not to put up defensive walls.

The conversation that follows might provide an opportunity to express your point of view, as well. If the other person shows an interest, then you can calmly explain why you believe as you do. You might have noticed that the two of you have some of the same values and have chosen different paths to accomplish similar outcomes. That shared vision for your lives provides a common ground on which understanding can be built – perhaps, even a closer relationship.

Which brings us to the heart of the issue – there is no good guy or bad guy, just two people who disagree.

## Remembering our Kinship

Our perspective in life comes from our life experience, but most of us do want to have our basic needs met and to have the freedom to express who we are, to be respected, and to have love and joy in our lives. This is an opportunity to look for common ground.

We can look at the areas in which we do agree - the kind of world we want for ourselves and our children and grandchildren. "I see this issue differently, but I believe we both want the same things in life," is a good way to begin

As we realize that we share a common vision, we find that we have common ground on which to build mutual respect, or even a relationship. We might go our separate ways, feeling better about each other than we would have previously. Sometimes, we actually find a friend where before we saw a foe.

In the process, we have discovered our kinship and stepped away from the ideas of "them" and "us." We have grown our circle of compassion to include someone previously on the outside, and we now see the power of curiosity to open doors of understanding.

We truly live the words of the song when we realize that we can do away with the idea of good guys and bad guys, and just see co-travelers on the journey of life, each of us doing the best we know how to do in the moment.

As a result, life just got richer.
We're grateful that you are on this journey with us.
With love from our hearts to yours,
*Pat and Larry*

# Is Peace Possible in Today's World?

*Kindness is the golden chain by which*
*society is bound together.*
~ Johann Wolfgang von Goethe

A song was a part of my growing up years, and it became a part of who I am. It invites us to contribute to the creation of peace in the world. This can seem overwhelming if we think about how insignificant we each are amidst millions of people, but it is empowering if we understand that we all have an impact on the world immediately around us by every action we take.

We all have been longing for peace in our lives, wanting to live in a world of kindness, cooperation, and mutual support. At this time in our history, such an idea seems impossible. By focusing on the smaller world of our daily lives, we can move out of disbelief into the realm of possibility. That's where everything begins – with us.

The key to peace is remembering that we are related to each other, even those we do not yet know. That requires us to expand the way we view each other, enlarging our circle of kinship.

Let's begin with our daily lives – with family, neighbors, co-workers, and those we meet casually during the day. Everyone has stresses in their lives, so we can begin by adding a little kindness to smooth the way a bit.

When we're stressed or frustrated with what is going on in our lives or in the world around us, we tend to be short-tempered and impatient with each other. We can begin there. We can decide to give each other a break and not react unkindly when someone releases their frustration on us.

So, how do we do that when we're stressed, too?

It takes practice, but we CAN do it, if it's important to us. It begins with recognizing that the unkind words coming at us is the other person releasing some of their stress on us. I've done that myself – taken out my frustration on people close to me. Remembering that makes it easier for me to understand what someone else is feeling.

With that awareness, it is easier to respond with kindness. Instead of reacting with a negative retort, we can reply with a kind remark, or even just ignore a negative comment.

We can even extend kindness to people who hold different political views. I know this is hard for most of us these days, but that may be the arena in which we most desperately need kindness.

It is hard to disregard the conflict and hostility that is growing in the world around us. We care about issues that trigger anger – in ourselves as well as others. I am not suggesting that we stop caring about those issues. I won't stop caring and speaking out about my vision of the way forward.

But we can live more peacefully with those who hold opposite views. We can see beyond politics. We can choose to see each other as whole human beings, all wanting a good life for ourselves and our families. We can also wonder about others - who they are in their daily lives.

One of our best friends holds political views opposite from ours, and he is one of the kindest people we know. If all we knew about him were his politics, we would not have imagined he could be a good friend. How much we would have missed out on by that judgment.

We live our daily lives moment by moment. They provide the opportunities to practice kindness when others are acting with impatience or even anger. I know from experience that even kind people are sometimes impatient and short-tempered. Imagine how much they would appreciate a kind word instead of a harsh reply.

It is not just the actions of others that cause negative responses in us. We are sometimes triggered by our judgments of how some people show up in our lives. A homeless person sleeping in our neighborhood is seen as a threat rather than a brother or sister who needs a little compassion. An angry person shouting in a store near us is seen as dangerous, but perhaps is just crying out for help. How can we reframe the way we see each other?

When we remember that we are all part of the human family, we are better able to wonder about others. What is happening in their life? What trauma and pain has led them to this behavior? What do they need that they are not getting?

Wondering helps us to have compassion, no matter how a person is behaving. I am reminded of a quote from Father Greg Boyle, "How do we achieve a compassion that allows us to stand in awe of what the poor have to carry rather than stand in judgment of how they carry it?"

This is asking a lot. Can we do this?

There is no right or wrong way, and there is no timer clicking away, measuring our progress. We each need to find our own way of meeting this opportunity to expand our kindness practice. It is a journey, and we each walk it the best way we know how.

But it helps to remember that every time we respond to others with kindness, we are adding to the peace in the world - with every thought, every act.

We're grateful that you are on this journey with us.

With love from our hearts to yours,

*Pat and Larry*

## Kindness Makes Us Happier

*"If you want others to be happy, practice compassion.*
*If you want to be happy, practice compassion."*
Dalai Lama

I had an experience this week that expanded my appreciation of the power of a simple act of kindness. Part of my journey has been to look for opportunities to say a few words of kindness to strangers – not just in person, but also when I'm on the phone.

I was speaking with an AT&T support person who was helping us resolve an issue with our phone service. She was very helpful. After previous attempts to solve the problem by two other people, she actually knew what to do, and we were relieved and grateful to her. I told her, "Thank you. You are very good at what you do, and I appreciate your help."

After a pause, she said, quietly, "Thank you so much. You make my heart happy."

Hearing her response made MY heart happy. A simple thank you is always good, and it would have been followed by "You're welcome," as a normal courtesy. Taking the time for a few extra words of appreciation opened the door for a deeper impact, and we were Both happier.

We all know that we feel happy when people are kind to us, but we also feel good when we are kind. A newly published review of decades of kindness research concluded that people who were kind tended to be healthier and happier. They found that people who performed random, informal acts of kindness, like sitting with a friend going through a hard time, tended to be happier than people who performed more formal acts of kindness, like volunteering with a local charity. This is not to suggest that we do not feel good when we volunteer, but apparently, we get an extra energetic boost when we perform spontaneous acts of kindness.

The researchers also found that people who were kind experienced "eudaimonic happiness" (a sense of meaning and purpose in life) rather than "hedonic happiness" (a sense of pleasure and comfort). People who were kind tended to have higher self-esteem and, to a lesser degree, they also experienced less depression and anxiety, and even improved physical health (among older adults). Researcher Elizabeth Midlarsky of Columbia University concluded that the research showed that being kind may make us feel better about ourselves, distract us from our own troubles, and help us be more socially connected with others.

It seems as if the chemistry in our bodies conspires to support and encourage kindness. When we are kind or when we receive or witness kindness, we get a rush of chemicals, including serotonin and endorphins (the body's "feel good chemicals"), and oxytocin (the "tend and befriend hormone"). Together, they enhance our feeling of wellbeing, increase our bonding to one another, and make us feel happy.

That, alone, is enough to entice us to find new ways to spread kindness in our daily lives.

Enjoy your journey!

We're grateful that you are on this journey with us.

With love from our hearts to yours,

*Pat and Larry*

## How Do You Want to Show Up in the World?

*"A vision is not just a picture of what could be;*
*it is an appeal to our better selves,*
*a call to become something more"*
... Rosabeth Moss Kanter

As we observe and participate in our world today, sometimes we wonder how we got to this point of division. But when we stop to consider the larger picture, we realize that the powerful force of love and kindness is showing up all around us, as an antidote to separation and even hatred.

So many people are living their lives with kindness and concern for others that it is easy to see our vision of a kinder, more peaceful world emerging around us. It is not just whimsical thinking. We know it is possible – not overnight, but over time - as more and more of us decide to live our lives with love and compassion, seeing no stranger, but remembering that we are all family.

Many of us feel called to be the change we want to see in the world, but how do we do that?

We do it by bringing awareness to every action we take as we go through our day, and then deciding if it is adding to or working against our vision of the world that we want to live in.

We each get to ask what we are being called to do in our daily lives. For many of us, walking a kindness path is answering that call. Our kindness practice not only enriches our lives, but it also enriches the world we live in.

We all have within us the potential for anger, fear, hatred, intolerance. It's easy to get angry, to be offended, to judge the other person as wrong and to react according to that idea. We also have within us love, non-judgment, and compassion.

When we choose to live with kindness, we are choosing to stop reacting out of fear, judgment, or anger. When those feelings arise, we can acknowledge them, but make a clear decision not to let them run our lives.

## There is a Cherokee parable:

An old chief was teaching his grandson about life…

"A fight is going on inside me," he said to the boy.

"It is a terrible fight, and it is between two wolves.

One is filled with anger, envy, greed, arrogance, resentment, self-pity, and lies.

The other is full of joy, peace, love, hope, humility, kindness, compassion, truth and faith.

This same fight is going on inside you – and inside every other person, too."

The grandson thought about it for a minute and then asked his grandfather,

"Which wolf will win?"

The old chief simply replied,

"The one you feed."

## We all get to choose which one we feed.

Most of us feed both wolves as we go through our daily lives. We're human. We're living in a challenging world. People and circumstances trigger us, and it's easy to react rather than responding thoughtfully.

We do have the ability to decide how we will respond, rather than reacting by habit. But habits are strong. So how do we move from reacting to a more thoughtful, kinder way of responding to others?

It requires us to have a clear intention to do so – and a vision of how we want to show up in the world.

Then, we need to pay attention, notice our reactions, and catch ourselves when we are adding to a difficult situation rather than easing it. This is not a way of making us feel bad that we didn't do better. It's a way of becoming aware and intending to respond in a better way next time.

**There is no right or wrong on the kindness path.**

It is a journey, and each step takes us further along the path.

Sometimes we encounter obstacles – challenges that are more difficult to overcome. Some people really push our buttons more than others. Sometimes, we feel so passionately about a situation that we see people who disagree with us as enemies rather than good people who have different ideas than we do.

It's easy to fall back into habitual reactions of anger or judgment or defensiveness. This is a challenge for most of us, but also an opportunity to shift our perspective. We can see one another as fellow humans, each on our own life journey – and realize that we have each become who we are as a result of our life experiences and the influence of the people in our lives and the ideas that we have been exposed to.

When we decide to show up in the world with kindness, we give each other a break. We look past our differences and find common ground on which to connect in a friendly way.

It may be easier to begin with neutral encounters. We can move from the easier friendly greeting for a stranger in the grocery store to the more challenging kind greeting for a person who is being rude. Then, with more time, we can find understanding and develop compassion for those we see now as our opponents.

**Step by step. Be patient with yourself.**

Ask yourself which wolf you are feeding today.

Love both wolves. They are both a part of you.

Then gently feed the one you want to show up in the world.

We're grateful that you are on this journey with us.

With love from our hearts to yours,

*Pat and Larry*

# Kindness is Love with Its Work Boots On

*Kindness is Love with Its*
*Work Boots On*
from "The House Bunny" movie

When Larry first read this quote, he came to me all excitedly, because it so clearly represented our idea that kindness is more than a nice feeling about other people. It demands that we take action and put it into practice in our daily lives.

Kindness is not a wishy-washy feeling that leads people to give in to others no matter what they say or do. It demands that we take a stand for what we see as good. It asks us to get off the couch and out in the world and carry the power of love into whatever challenging or messy situation we encounter. It means bringing light and love into places of darkness. It means encouraging and uplifting the people we encounter.

Sometimes being kind is easy, a natural part of our day. We smile at a stranger or say something pleasant to the check-out person in a store. Sometimes it requires us to get up earlier or to give up some leisure time so we can help at a local charity or help a neighbor who lives alone and can't easily get out to the store or just needs someone to sit and keep her company for a while.

Sometimes it means being courageous – taking a stand that is not popular or that involves some risk. Taking a stand is not always easy. It may expose us to ridicule, verbal abuse from people who disagree, or the loss of a friend. But when we are serious about living with kindness, we understand the power we have to make a difference in the world, and we always get to choose the right path for us.

Sometimes kindness means listening to others in order to understand them, and respecting them, even when their ideas or world views are different from ours. At this time, when our world seems to be more divided than before, many of us are being defined by one idea or belief or group that we belong to.

We seem to have forgotten how to see each other as the

whole, complex people that we are. We can rise above that easy, quick tendency to reject each other by remembering those things that we share – a desire to live in a peaceful world in which our needs are met, our natural tendency to be kind, and the universal need to live with love in our lives.

### Kindness in the Pandemic

At this time, in the middle of a pandemic, we have had unlimited opportunities to step up and help one another. The internet has been indispensable – a way to stay in touch and support one another when we could not get together in person.

Stories from all over the world have demonstrated how kindness is a natural human inclination. People have looked for ways to help those in their community- running errands for those who cannot, checking in by phone or in person to support one another, collecting and distributing needed food or other items for those in need.

At the same time, the internet has been a means of spreading ideas that separate us and make enemies out of people who have different ideas. If we are truly living as love with our work boots on, we can take a stand against those ideas that divide us. We can listen to each other in order to understand, not to condemn, one another. We can remember and remind others of all that we still have in common.

Love asks a lot from us, and we are up to it.

We thank you for putting on your work boots and taking your love out into the world. Together, we really are making our world a kinder, more loving place.

We're grateful that you are on this journey with us.

With love from our hearts to yours,

*Pat and Larry*

# Kindness Is More Than an Action

*After a while, kindness is not just an act you're doing.*
*It becomes who you are.*

Nipun Mehta

Most people are kind in their daily activities, given circumstances that are comfortable and with people who are familiar. We find it easy to greet each other and say a few words of acknowledgement. These are acts of kindness that make the day more pleasant for everyone involved, and they provide a strong platform on which we can expand the reach of our kindness.

The challenge is finding a way to be kind to people outside of our comfort zone – people who seem to be different from us, who are harder for us to relate to. We often have unconscious reasons to be uneasy or we hold judgments that prevent us from reaching out to them.

What we do know, if we stop for a moment to think about it, is that we do not know enough about others to shut them out. So why do we hesitate?

**It isn't about them. It's about us.**

If we want to live in a kind world, then we get to demonstrate in our lives what that world would look like.

We get to ask ourselves, "Who do I want to be?"

Many people feel no desire to expand their circle of kindness. That's okay. They are still making a difference in the world with every act of kindness.

For some people, kindness is not just a way of acting in the world. They want it to be a way of being. For them, over time, it becomes who they are.

That doesn't happen overnight. It requires us to find within us the courage to let other people into our life.

It becomes easier to reach out when we realize that we are each on a unique life path but sharing the same need for acceptance from others.

Changing from an old, habitual way of reacting to others

takes practice. It doesn't happen in a day.

**How do we get there from where we are right now**?

It begins with having an intention to live with kindness in all our encounters, then holding that vision as we go through our day.

It means letting go of our judgments, and accepting people as they are.

It means rising above an old habit of reacting to others, and acting as the person we have chosen to be.

It means expressing kindness in all our encounters, without requiring people to "deserve it."

It means simply being kind and ignoring the logical reasons that try to dissuade us.

It means silently asking in all encounters, "How can I show up here with love and compassion?"

It means remembering the bigger picture – we are all flawed human beings, each doing the best we know how at this moment, and we're in this life together for a reason.

When we embody kindness, we intend to live with love, compassion and non-judgment – in our thoughts, our words and our actions.

None of us will accomplish this all the time. But living with that intention, we will move closer to it with practice. It is a journey without end. Let it be an adventure

When we make that choice, we have the exquisite joy of being kind.

It becomes who we are.

We're grateful that you are on this journey with us.

With love from our hearts to yours,

*Pat and Larry*

## The Power of Small Acts of Kindness

*Great opportunities to help others seldom come,*
*but small ones surround us every day.*
Sally Koch – Author

We often hear about organizations that are having a positive impact on the world, and we may be inspired to support their work, through our financial contributions or by offering our time as a volunteer. There is power in coming together to help others.

As we consider the impact of our individual acts of kindness, we may feel that, by contrast, we individually, cannot make much of a difference in the world.

I see it differently. I believe that the cumulative effect of our daily small actions is the foundation on which we are building a safer and more compassionate world. If we each reach out with friendliness or support to another person every day, the cumulative effect will be immeasurable. We will never know the impact on the individual receiving our kindness, and then the ripple effect, as they pass it on through the day, as a result of the uplift it gave them.

There are so many ways to acknowledge others or to show appreciation for them. If we go out into our day with the intention of spreading kindness, opportunities appear with everyone we encounter. These lead to unplanned actions, determined by each situation.

You already have your own way of being kind, so you know how good it feels. Here are a few ideas that may inspire you to expand your kindness practice.

### Spontaneous Acts of Kindness

Smile at anyone you meet, whether they respond or not. They usually will.

Make a sincere compliment to someone you encounter - perhaps the receptionist or another person in the waiting room with you. I enjoy telling people what a great smile they have – but only if they really do.

Ask the name of a worker at a store or in an office that you visit regularly and then, greet them by name each time you see them.

Make a comment of appreciation for anyone who helps you – a cashier in a store, a nurse in a doctor's office, even the person restocking shelves at the grocery store.

Notice someone who is struggling and may need help opening a door, getting out of a chair or putting groceries in the car - then step up to help.

Greet other people in a waiting room or in line at a store with a pleasant comment, then see what conversation may follow.

Ignore a rude comment, or respond with one that is kind, assuming that the other person is having a bad day.

Each situation will provide a chance to respond in a kind way.

### Planned Acts of Kindness

Family, friends, and neighbors provide many opportunities for kind acts. Do you have a skill that will help a friend through a challenge? Does someone need help with shopping, a ride to a doctor or help with yard work? Does a neighbor who lives alone need a friendly ear and caring heart?

Ask what you can do to help, and you may be pleasantly surprised by the chance it gives you to connect in a deeper way.

Birthday cards or ecards and messages of congratulation on an anniversary or graduation are a good way to connect with people we don't see often. Thank you notes, after receiving a gift, give us a way of acknowledging the kindness of others.

Do you have an old friend or a distant family member that you haven't connected with lately? Perhaps, a phone call - or a pleasant email greeting - would brighten the day for both of you. Make a list of people you have not talked with in a while, and you will be surprised at how many opportunities it gives you to reach out.

Many organizations providing services to less fortunate members of our community need contributions of clothing, household items, toys, and other items for children. That provides us a good way to pass on items that we no longer use and to brighten the day for someone else.

As we continue on our kindness journey, we notice the people around us, and we find new opportunities to reach out to them. We become more creative in our response, and we get to experience the joy of finding new ways to take our love out into the world.

Our wish for you is that you have fun on your journey.

We're grateful that you are on this journey with us.

With love from our hearts to yours,

*Pat and Larry*

# The Life-Changing Power of Gratitude

*When we focus on our gratitude,*
*the tide of disappointment goes out,*
*and the tide of love rushes in.*

Kristin Armstrong

In her TED Talk, Hailey Bartholomew describes her journey from feeling emotionally disconnected from her life to discovering "the secret to happiness." It is a funny, moving, and inspiring story.

Hailey was unable to enjoy life. The daily routines of being a wife and mother felt "blah" and seemed to have no meaning for her. She wanted to feel gratitude for her life, but she was not able to feel anything.

While looking for someone who could help her get out of the doldrums, she was guided to a woman who helped her to see her life in a totally new light. She received an insight that changed her life: "The secret to happiness is reflection and gratitude."

Hailey was to spend 10 minutes every evening reflecting on the day, noticing anything that made her feel grateful. She began to see things that she had not noticed before, and soon, she was feeling gratitude for small moments in her life.

That experience inspired her to go on a photographic journey, and she decided to take a photograph every day of something that she was grateful for. She began her 365 Grateful Project, which changed her life in ways she could not have imagined. Her journey showed her that her expectations of other people had kept her from appreciating them, and her relationships improved. She tells a moving story about her husband.

Hailey learned that even in the hard things in life, we can choose to be grateful. Now, she will tell you that gratitude has helped her to learn from everything happening in her life and to find "the gold in the mud."

I invite you to enjoy her uplifting TED Talk. It inspired me and I believe it will do the same for you.

We're grateful that you are on this journey with us.

Pat Downing

With love from our hearts to yours,
*Pat and Larry*

## Love is What the World Needs Now

*I have decided to stick to love…*
*Hate is too great a burden to bear.*
Martin Luther King, Jr.

I remember a song that was a part of my life for a few years while I was in college in the 1960s. The words really spoke to me. "What the world needs now is love, sweet love. That's the only thing that there's just too little of."

That was a time when our country was deeply divided – thousands of people protesting against racial discrimination at home and an unpopular war in Vietnam, and supporters of the status quo labeling the protestors as unpatriotic and dangerous.

Fast forward to today. Once again, our country is deeply divided, and we desperately need a lot more love and a lot less hatred and refusal to even listen to each other.

We have allowed political views to solidify into intractable positions of "I am right, and you are wrong, I am a good guy, and you are an enemy." As a country, we have turned the idea of brotherhood into one of "us and them."

How did we get to this ugly place once again?

I believe that we forgot how to love each other. Love does not mean agreeing on everything. It means working to understand each other and to find common ground on which to build a future together.

Often, we don't give ourselves the opportunity to get to know people we disagree with. We see them as those people who are against me.

The Sufi poet, Rumi, shed some light on this:

*Your task is not to seek for love, but merely to seek and find*
*all the barriers*
*within yourself that you have built against it.*

That calls for some self-reflection. I realize that so much of what shows up in our lives is a result of the lens through which we view others. As hard as it is for us to look at, we do have to admit that we build barriers to love when we see people who disagree with us are our enemies. That puts up a wall between them and us that prevents us from even trying to understand each other.

So, step one is to turn judgment into curiosity. Why do they think that way? What do they really want for their lives? Can we find common ground?

Paul Tillich answers these with a simple formula:

*The first duty of love is to listen.*

How do we even begin to answer these questions if we are not even talking to each other?

The Black musician, Daryl Davis, provides an example. He has made it his mission to befriend people in hate groups like the Klu Klux Klan by calmly confronting them with the question: "How can you hate me if you don't even know me?"

"Give them a platform, he said. "You challenge them. But you don't challenge them rudely or violently. You do it politely and intelligently. And when you do things that way, chances are they will reciprocate and give you a platform."

That leads to the discovery of the common ground you both stand on - values, hopes for the future, what you really want for your lives. Once you find out that you agree on many issues, the barriers come down and you no longer see each other as enemies.

Daryl's efforts resulted in several clansmen becoming his friend and giving up their clan membership. Our challenge is a bit different, but the message is the same. When we take down the barriers in ourselves that prevent us from getting to know people who disagree with us, we find that we have more in common than we thought.

Of course, most of us do not have the time or inclination to go out and engage people one-on-one in conversation about our different views. But we can begin by accepting the idea that we do have a lot in common. We are all individuals, and we cannot be painted by the same brush, which is colored by the ideas in someone else's head about who we are.

As Jim Krueger reminds us, in the song made famous by Dave Mason,

> *There ain't no good guy, there ain't no bad guy.*
> *There's only you and me, and we just disagree.*

We do have the power to let go of judgments about each other and to remind ourselves that we are probably more alike than we thought. Then we will remember how to love each other and begin to build a better future together.

Love is what the world needs now, and it's ours to give. Let's expand and deepen our kindness journey and flood the world with love, sweet love.

Wishing you joy on your journey.

We're grateful that you are on this journey with us.

With love from our hearts to yours,

*Pat and Larry*

# Adventures with a Mouse and a Kind Community

*The greatness of a nation can be judged by the way
its animals are treated.*
~ Mahatma Gandhi

This is a story of the kindness of strangers that demonstrates the power of community.

We believe that most people are kind, and our experiences continue to support that belief. Most people do care about each other and reach out to help someone in need.

We are fortunate to belong to the Nextdoor online platform that enables neighbors to communicate with each other. Membership is free. As people post information of interest or ask for assistance with a personal or community need, nearby members receive emails with links to the posts. If we click on a link, we can make a comment, and we receive updates as other people comment on that post.

This is a powerful tool for building community among people who do not usually have opportunities to meet otherwise. By following the thread of a post, we learn more about our neighbors, and we have the opportunity to help others or to participate in a community activity.

This week, we experienced the power of Nextdoor, and it is a wonderful example of the kindness of strangers. In order to demonstrate how deeply people get involved in helping a stranger solve a problem, I decided to share our experience with some detail.

A few days ago, we realized that we had an uninvited guest. After hearing unexplained noises during the day, we finally spotted a mouse scurrying across the floor. I posted a request for help on Nextdoor: "Does anyone know where we can get a live mouse trap in Asheville?"

Almost immediately, someone posted a helpful suggestion that peppermint oil on cotton balls would run them out. I thanked her and explained that, in our situation, we need to provide a way out. The mouse apparently came in through an open door to the house from the carport. It does not have a way to get out without our help. We intended to catch and release it outside

That exchange was followed by suggestions from several people about where to find humane mouse traps. One was from a couple who had taken the time to research for us and sent us a screen capture from the website of our local Home Depot with several choices.

Other people replied to posted suggestions, agreeing and sometimes offering their ideas as well. One woman wrote that her son was like a ninja and he would be able to catch our intruder and release it outside. It's hard to turn down such an appealing offer. I replied that I would enjoy meeting a ninja, but we think the humane mouse traps will do the trick.

We received several ideas for catching a mouse without a trap. One uses fishnet. Another requires a bucket, newspaper and peanut butter. The simplest one uses the flexible hose from a vacuum cleaner. The fourth one calls for an empty cereal box, and the last one was fanciful, using a swinging-top trash can, a ruler and some peanut butter. It has been a serious – and amusing - education in mouse-catchery.

We also received words of wisdom – "A house isn't a house without a mouse." And then came the inevitable suggestion that we borrow a cat.

Five people offered to loan us their humane catch and release mouse traps. We were willing to drive to pick up the traps, and one woman offered to bring them to us. At that point, we were overwhelmed by the kindness coming to us from all directions.

When Erin arrived, we all felt that we were meant to meet – and it took a wayward mouse to bring us together. We smile when we think about the unpredictable ways that synchronicity works in our lives.

Well, the traps were great, but our little mouse was just a tad too big to fit in the opening. She was frustrated and so were we. So back to Nextdoor to share an update on our on-going adventure. This time, Julie responded, and she also insisted on coming to our house to deliver her traps.

The mouse wouldn't go into another trap with peanut butter, apparently remembering her experience with the last one. When we realized that and replaced the peanut butter with cheese, she eventually went in and could not get back out.

Success feels so good after the twists and turns of the last few days. Larry released our visitor back to her home territory, and we are optimistic that she won't want to come back inside. We are certainly going to be more careful about leaving doors open.

This entire journey was made possible by the Nextdoor platform. Yes, we would have resolved the issue sooner if we had just bought a trap, but we gained so much by involving our neighbors in our mouse adventure. We felt embraced by many people we now see as friends we have not yet met in person.

Nextdoor provides an easy way for people to express and to receive kindness. Given the opportunity, many people quickly respond to someone in need. We encourage anyone with a problem or a challenge to reach out to your neighbors for help. The experience will enrich your life and theirs.

Kindness abounds!

We're grateful that you are on this journey with us.

With love from our hearts to yours,

*Pat and Larry*

## Joy is a Journey

*Joy is what happens to us when we allow ourselves
to recognize how good things really are.*
                                                    Marianne Williams

This is a season of joy. Festive lights and holiday music proclaim celebration, and we are reminded that this is a special time.

Of course, sharing gifts and holiday meals are part of how we celebrate, and that celebration brings us joy. But it is so easy to get caught up in the preparation of gifts and decorations and elaborate holiday meals that we often forget to enjoy the process.

Joy can be the exuberant expression of happiness. It can also be a quiet experience of delight or appreciation.

It may seem that we just don't have time for joy in the midst of our busy holiday preparations, but it just requires a shift of focus. Whatever you are doing, stop and look around you. What beauty do you see? Take a moment to appreciate it – festive decorations, the smile on someone's face, the hustle and bustle of other people engaged in their preparations for celebration.

Waiting in a checkout line, use the time to think of the blessings in your life, and turn impatience to get on to the next thing on your list into a moment of gratitude.

Look at the sky and feel the warmth of the sun on your face.

Notice the people passing by, and silently wish them well.

As someone approaches you, nod and smile. You will uplift their day, and yours, too.

Greet the checkout person or other store workers with a smile and pleasant greeting. A few words of appreciation will provide a bright spot in their busy day.

Lighten up a chore at home by listening to holiday music or other uplifting music you love.

As you are preparing a meal or gifts for the special people in your life, think of them while you go through the motions, adding your love into the mix.

Your experiences will offer you unique opportunities for joy. Look for them and enjoy them.

Of course, the greatest joy is the time of sharing our gifts and good food and the delight of being together in love and appreciation for one another.

When we have experienced joy in the process of preparation, this time will not be just a few moments of joy. It will be the final celebration of a journey of joy.

We're grateful that you are on this journey with us.

With love from our hearts to yours,

*Pat and Larry*

## Seeing Beauty Everywhere

*Everything has beauty,*
*but not everyone sees it.*
Confucius

At this time of year, we pause our daily routines for celebration and remembrance of the deeper meaning of our lives. We decorate our homes and play seasonal music, creating an atmosphere of joy and beauty.

As we go out in the world around us, we see the results of the efforts of others to celebrate with lights and decorations on their homes and in their businesses. We seem to have a natural inclination to create beauty as part of our celebration of life. Beauty gives us joy, and it is also an expression of our joy.

It's easy to see beauty when it's right in front of us making a clear statement that today is special. But how easily do we see the beauty in our ordinary, daily lives?

*Beauty is everywhere.*
*You only have to look to see it.*

Bob Ross

We get so caught up in the routines of our lives that we don't take the time to notice the beauty all around us.

I remember, over 40 years ago, walking one morning with my daughter, Christie, in a stroller. I stopped in front of a yard with a single flower in full bloom right by the street. Christie's face lit up with a big smile as she looked at me and pointed to the flower. I had walked past that flower during my early morning walk, and I had not noticed it. With my head full of plans for the day, I had missed the gift in front of me.

How often do we forget to be present in the moments of our lives, to look around us and see what beauty is surrounding us?

Do we believe that beauty is everywhere – or is that just in the imagination of a dreamer who is disconnected from real life?

I can't answer that question for you, but I began looking for my own answer – and what I discovered surprised me.

As I began noticing, I realized that I had been living disconnected from my world with my lack of attention. I went through my days living in my head, and I missed so many of the gifts that the world offered me.

As I learned to become more present, especially while walking, I saw beauty all around me, often in the little things that I had taken for granted – the pattern of colored leaves on the ground, the play of light and shadow across a building, the beautiful symmetry of the limbs and branches of a maple tree in winter, and the equally beautiful lack of symmetry of a weeping cherry tree, whose limbs seemed to have minds of their own.

The more I became enchanted with the world around me, the more it revealed its beauty to me.

I began to feel deep gratitude for the little things that I now noticed, and it enriched my life in unexpected ways.

Over time, I began seeing beauty in other people I encountered during my day. As I developed the habit of smiling as we approached each other, they often responded in kind, and then, for a moment, we shared the quiet joy of connection. It didn't matter who they were or how they looked – a shopper in a store or a homeless person on the street. The acknowledgement of a smile has magic in it.

Beauty surrounds us, and it also exists inside us. We are in charge of how much we let in and how much we are willing to share with others. That choice has an impact on the quality of our lives.

Our wish for you is that your life is filled with beauty and the joy that comes from it.

We're grateful that you are on this journey with us.

With love from our hearts to yours,

*Pat and Larry*

## Happiness and Kindness Dance Together

*Remember that the happiest people are not those getting more, but those giving more.*

Jackson Brown, Jr

A few weeks ago, a contagiously happy woman came bubbling into our life, and we want you to meet her. Kelli Pease hosts the Happsters website, and she nurtures and shares her happiness through her blogs and simple practices that help her to stay happy, no matter what else is going on in her life. Kelli created a practice that she calls the "Happsters Weekly 3." She has found that rituals keep her focused and grounded, and this one is a simple and effective way to stay in the happiness zone throughout the week:

- Every Sunday, I pull out an index card and divide it into 3 sections: MONDAY INTENTION // WEDNESDAY GRATITUDE // FRIDAY JOY
- On Monday mornings, I write what my intention is for the week under "Monday Intention."
- On Wednesday mornings, I write 3 things I'm grateful for in that moment.
- On Friday mornings, I write a simple thing that I'm looking forward to that day. It's always something that I think will bring me joy. Sometimes it's more than 1 thing!
- (OPTIONAL) At the end of the week, I snap a photo and text it to one of my friends and she sends me hers.

Kelli believes that happiness comes from focusing on the 4 Gs: Gratitude, Growth, Giving & Gathering, so she focuses on these four elements in her life and in her writing. In our conversation, she shared with us about the role they play in her life and how kindness is an important part of her life.

## Kindness

I believe that being kind to others contributes greatly to our happiness. When we make others happy through acts of kindness, it gives us an instant boost. Just smiling at a stranger on the street can create an energy exchange that feeds both you and the other person. In fact when I used to run women's happiness groups a few years ago, the members would always tell me their favorite activity was when we gave away flowers to people walking by on the street. We did all kinds of activities in our events, but practicing kindness and giving to others was consistently the thing that brought us all the most joy. When we practice gratitude, growth, giving and gathering regularly, it naturally brings joy and happiness to our lives.

## Gratitude

There's a reason why writing down what you're grateful for has become so trendy. Practicing gratitude has been linked to an increase in happiness and a decrease in depression. I've found that when I switch up what I'm grateful for each day, it's even more effective in increasing my happiness. So instead of consistently writing down that you're thankful for "family" or "friends," try to challenge yourself to come up with some other things you're grateful for. Is the sun shining? Is your couch super comfortable? The more thought you give it, the more you'll come up with great things you have in your life to be thankful for.

My favorite gratitude practices to do regularly include thinking of what I'm grateful for as I'm falling asleep at night, starting off Monday mornings by writing down the people, places and things I'm grateful for, and mailing unexpected thank you notes to people who have made a difference in my life.

## Growth

When I talk about growth in the 4G's of happiness, I'm really referring to focusing on having a growth mindset, being curious, and learning new things. People who have a growth mindset (instead of a fixed mindset) tend to be happier and more at peace than those who have a fixed mindset. One of the most important aspects of my own growth has been the realization that everyone goes through setbacks in life and it's how you handle them that really matters. The key for me is to not let those knock me down and instead challenge myself to look for the lesson in each one. Journaling has really helped me to find the hidden lessons along the way. Other ways I include growth into my life include reading personal development books and taking courses about topics I'm interested in. Finally, practicing mindfulness has been a large part of my growth journey and it's very important for me to have a consistent morning routine that includes some kind of meditation practice.

## Giving

"The Joy of Giving" isn't just a popular phrase! Giving really does bring joy and happiness. A 2017 study found that people are happier overall when they give to others and that the more that people give, the happier they tend to be. I was so inspired by how much my women's group loved giving and receiving flowers (as mentioned previously) that last year I set out on a mission to give away one million flowers. I now have a cut flower garden and have an amazing local market that donates flowers to the cause. I still have a ways to go until I hit one millions flowers, but I won't ever get tired of seeing the joy it brings to the recipients.

## Gathering

Loneliness is at an all-time high right now with the rise of COVID. Unfortunately, it has been harder than ever to maintain friendships and gather with people in real life lately, but we all crave connection and friendship and need it for our health and happiness. In fact, friends become increasingly important to health and happiness as people age, according to research in the journal Personal Relationships. Even if it's a virtual form of getting together, anything helps! I regularly gather with friends and family and make that time together a priority in my life. When possible, I host gatherings at my house around certain topics that I know we're all interested in. Sometimes we'll have a full moon circle and talk about astrology, and other times we have taco-rating parties, where we order tacos from a few different restaurants and rate all of their elements to find the best taco in San Diego. Good times! The important part is that we're all together and as present as possible.

Thinking about the 4 G's at the beginning of each week has been a great way for me to center and remember about what I value in life. It's easy to get caught up in the day-to-day and the 4 G's have been an amazing anchor for me.

We appreciate Kelli for sharing her heart with us and for sharing new ways that we can bring more happiness and kindness into our lives.

We're grateful that you are on this journey with us.

With love from our hearts to yours,

*Pat and Larry*

## The Many Languages of Love

*All the people you haven't told you love lately,*
*tell them and live your days like you mean it.*
Hal Sutton

There are many ways that we can express kindness in our relationships.

Gary Chapman is an American pastor and relationship counselor. In his book, "The 5 Love Languages," he describes what he considers to be the five ways that people express love in a marriage or romantic relationship, and the love language that they need to receive in order to feel loved.

Although he writes about marriage or romantic relationships, we all express love in many other relationships – with family and friends, with co-workers, even in casual encounters with people we don't know as we go through our daily lives. So, let's consider how we can expand the way that we express kindness in those relationships as well.

Gary describes the five love languages as:
- Words of affirmation
- Quality time
- Giving and receiving gifts
- Acts of service
- Physical touch

Kindness is love in action. As we consider each love language, let's consider how we can bring more kindness into the expression of our love.

### Words of Affirmation

We all appreciate being acknowledged, not only for something we have done, but just for being who we are. Some people do not need verbal reassurance that they are loved, but for others, words are the language of love.

It is easy to express our love and appreciation in words:
- I love you.
- I appreciate all that you do for me.

- Just being with you makes me happy.
- Thank you for ... (be specific, preferably every day)
- You look great.
- I love you exactly as you are.

Words are especially important with children, whose view of themselves is created by the words of the adults in their lives. Thanking them, acknowledging small accomplishments, letting them know that you are glad to have them in your life – all help them to feel loved.

Kindness calls on us to be mindful of the words we speak in all relationships. While uplifting words strengthen our connection, words of criticism or mocking do the opposite.

## Quality Time

Quality is the key word here. That means doing something together that gets our full attention.

It can be as simple as:

- eating together while having conversations about the day,
- sharing memories - especially those that make you laugh,
- working on a jigsaw puzzle along with conversation,
- singing or playing musical instruments together.

Quality time with a child would be any enjoyable activity that engages them or helps them to feel empowered. Art projects, for instance, offer the opportunity to express their creativity and to experience the satisfaction of accomplishment.

Quality time means different things to different people.

Larry and I have a daily ritual of sharing time together over our morning coffee and tea. This is our time to talk about what is on our hearts and minds, to support one another, and to share our ideas on our current life journey.

Many families strengthen their bonds by hiking, camping or skiing together – creating good memories to enrich their future relationship. Others go for a walk together after a meal. The key is to engage with one another being fully present, not being distracted by thoughts of what else you could be doing.

### Giving and Receiving Gifts

For some people, gifts convey a message that they are loved, and not receiving gifts carries the opposite message. For most women, flowers speak of love. For some, jewelry or special items of clothing are important.

Gifts for a man could be a book on his favorite subject, or an item of clothing that celebrates his favorite sports team. It might be a tool or equipment that would support his hobby or make his work around the house easier.

The monetary value of the gift is not as important as frequency. It takes a little creativity to come up with gifts on a regular basis. Cards or notes expressing appreciation cost little but may have a larger impact, especially if the message is a sincere expression of your love.

### Acts of Service

When acts of service are a primary expression of love, we demonstrate our love by our actions and, also by our expression of appreciation for the support we receive. For many people, going to a job and supporting a spouse or a family financially is their primary love language, which is often not acknowledged.

In many homes, each person has chores to attend to every day or every week. These are gifts to one another, but it is so easy to forget to thank each other for their contribution to the running of the household.

A kind gift could be to ask, "What can I do for you?" Sometimes what people need is obvious, and at other times, we have no idea what would be helpful right now. The other side of that coin is to gently ask for the help that would support you most in the moment.

Sometimes acts of service require a lot more from us, such as caregiving over a long period of time. That is a discussion for another post, but I know that such extended acts of service can bring unexpected gifts.

### Physical Touch

Romantic partners whose main love language is physical touch will feel loved when they kiss, hug, cuddle, have sex and hold each other after. Each of us place degrees of importance on the different ways of touching. The kind way to understand each other is to discuss your feelings and agree on a practice that meets the needs of both people.

Of course, touch is also important in non-romantic relationships.

It is especially true for children – sitting on someone's lap and feeling embraced, holding hands when out for a walk, a hug when leaving home or coming back later,

As adults, we still appreciate hugs from family or friends and sometimes we enjoy walking, holding hands or with our arms around each other. One expression of our love is reaching out and touching the arm of someone in need – making a physical connection that carries a message of support.

A handshake is a socially acceptable way of having physical contact in a more formal environment. Although it has become business protocol, it does express our need for connection. Even outside the business context, a handshake is a friendly way of welcoming someone.

## We are all different

Part of our kindness journey is to do what we can to understand and support the people in our lives. It is important to learn from them the best ways in which we can express our love to them.

This may mean having some gentle, honest conversations about each other's needs and preferences – setting ego aside and listening from our hearts. Then we will each have a roadmap to a more fulfilling journey together.

We're grateful that you are on this journey with us.

With love from our hearts to yours,

*Pat and Larry*

## Living with Kindness Is a Choice

*What you do makes a difference, and you have to decide what kind of difference you want to make.*
*- Jane Goodall -*

As Larry and I continue to explore what it means to us to live with kindness, we have discovered that there are several aspects of the kindness path that are defined by words that begin with the letter C.

Here is a good starting point:

## Choice

Choosing kindness is a choice of love over the fear and despair that cause many people to stop believing in their power to make a difference in the world, even in their own lives.

It is a conscious choice to be on a path of kindness, no matter how other people show up.

That choice for us is grounded in our vision of the world we want to live in. We have a vision of a better world in which more people live with kindness and consideration for each other. That has become the template for our lives today.

When we choose to live that way, our lives help to strengthen the power of love and kindness in the world. We uplift our own lives and the lives of those we encounter.

Being on a kindness path is not just about random acts of kindness. It is a choice to become the change we wish to see in the world. It is a conscious decision to live as love in action.

Think of yourself as love with its work boots on, not passively sitting at home thinking kind thoughts, but out in the world, bringing love with you wherever you go. When you make that choice, you engage the transformative power of love in your life.

When you choose a kindness path, you are not just choosing to act kindly. You are choosing to be kind because that becomes who you are. With that realization, you understand that it is never about how someone else is behaving. It is about you – who you choose to be.

## What is a Kindness Path?

We each walk a kindness path in our own unique way. There is no right or wrong way.

For some people, it means continuing their habit of small acts of kindness as they go through their day.

For some, it may mean expanding their circle of kindness to include people they had passed by but had not noticed before, as if they were just part of the background in their daily lives.

For some people, it may mean joining together with others by volunteering for an organization that is helping people meet their needs or enhance their lives in some way.

Each path makes a difference in their lives and in the world.

## Allowing Others

A key to walking any kindness path is choosing to allow other people to show up as they are. That means not overreacting to them, no matter how they behave.

When my daughter, Christie, was a pre-teen, she was with me in a store as I was checking out. I don't remember what was said, but I felt the cashier had been rude to me, and I was unkind in my response. I remember feeling a certain self-righteousness – How dare she talk to me that way!

I noticed Christie looked uncomfortable. When I asked her later about it, she told me she had been embarrassed. That was a wake-up call for me. It forced me to look at myself, and what I saw wasn't pretty.

I knew that I had to change my reactions to others. It has been a long process. I still catch myself reacting with annoyance or impatience from time to time, but I feel better, now, than I used to feel about how I usually show up in the world.

We do not go from reacting to allowing overnight. I have failed many times to respond with kindness. Our automatic reactions are habitual. Changing them takes time and a desire to change how we interact with others.

It helps me when I realize that I do not have enough information to judge others. I do not know their life story, and if I did, I would probably understand why they're making the choices that they are making now in their lives.

But I don't need to know their story. I can be kind because it is who I am – rather than being unkind, because of who I judge them to be.

We have to be patient with ourselves on this journey. It takes practice. But first it takes awareness. We start by noticing our own thoughts and feelings and how we express them. Then we notice the response of others to how we treat them.

It is a journey. We take one step at a time, as we're building a new habit. Notice how much better you feel when you bring kindness rather than annoyance with you when you go out in the world.

I invite you to choose your own kindness path and to explore with us, as we continue to share the rest of the 9 Cs of kindness.

We're grateful that you are on this journey with us.

With love from our hearts to yours,

*Pat and Larry*

## Commitment to Kindness Becomes a Way of Life

*The true meaning of life is to plant trees
under whose shade you do not expect to sit.*
Nelson Henderson

When we make the choice to live with kindness, we are choosing a way of life that invites us to think differently about how we meet each day. That choice brings with it a commitment to start where we are and to be more aware of opportunities to be kind as we go through our day.

## Planting Seeds

Every act of kindness is like a seed we are planting in our world, knowing that each one helps to create the kinder world that we envision. Often, we receive immediate feedback in the form of a smile or a pleasant comment in return, but sometimes, we do not get a response. It is helpful to remember that seeds need time to grow.

We are all planting seeds of some kind, and we get to decide what kind we're planting. When we choose seeds of kindness, in time, we will reap an abundant harvest in our lives, but we won't see the many others who will benefit in their lives from the seeds that we planted.

## Commitments to Ourselves

As we keep planting those seeds, it is helpful to develop habits that support expanding the reach of our kindness practice. We can make commitments to ourselves:

### To be aware of opportunities to be kind

A key to a satisfying kindness journey is staying conscious of the people around us. When we stay present in the moment, we notice people and we can see ways to respond to them with kindness.

It may be as simple as smiling and acknowledging someone or making a pleasant comment. It might be inviting someone behind in line to go ahead of us or stepping up to help someone by opening a door or carrying something for them. It may, at times, require more of us.

We get to decide in every encounter how to respond.

**To acknowledge kindness when we receive it or observe it**

There are no insignificant acts of kindness. For many people, small kind acts are their way of being in the world.

When we receive their kindness, it is easy to thank them. Beyond that courtesy, we like to say, "You are very kind," as an acknowledgment. Sometimes, we tell them our favorite definition of kindness – "Love with its work boots on," and then say, "That is you."

We each have our own way of receiving kindness. It is part of the joy of the kindness path.

**To graciously receive other people's kindness**

Many of us are so used to being self-sufficient that we automatically turn other people's kindness away. It is easy to reject an offer of help, saying, "I'm fine, thanks," even if a little help would be welcome. We do ourselves and the giver of kindness a favor when receiving their offer.

One evening, we were with friends at a local Waffle House restaurant. While we were enjoying our meal and each other's company, two men from the table behind me were leaving, and one of them presented me with a large feather, without a word. Taken by surprise, I thanked him, then he was gone before I could say anything else. To this day, that feather reminds me of the kindness of a stranger, and it has a special place on my desk.

Kindness is a circle, always in flow. If no one is willing to receive kindness, no one will be able to give it. I hope the stranger with the feather felt the joy that I experienced in receiving his gift.

As an aside: Larry says, "Remember to make an occasional trip to a Waffle House and mingle with the salt of Earth."

## To look honestly at ourselves

Setting time aside for reflection is helpful as we navigate our kindness path.

Looking back at the end of the day helps me to see:

- How I was kind and to whom,
- How it felt,
- Where I was hesitant to be kind and why,
- Who I am excluding from my kindness.
- What judgments in me prevent me from being kind.

I can ask myself,

- "What could I do next time to overcome the hesitance that prevented me from being kind this time.?
- "What am I afraid of?"
- "Why?"

This process of reflection helps us to understand ourselves better, so we can be more comfortable the next time life presents us with similar encounters. It helps us to decide when and how to expand the circle of our kindness.

## We each choose our level of commitment

There is no right or wrong way to walk a kindness path. We each get to choose our way of bringing love out into the world.

We invite you to commit to whatever level you are comfortable with. Then, when you are ready, you may want to take it up a notch – going from kindness in comfortable situations to those that are more challenging. It can be a bit scary, but also exhilarating when we step out of our comfort zone.

We thank you for choosing to bring your kindness out into a world that needs all the love it can get. You do make a difference with every act of kindness.

We're grateful that you are on this journey with us.

With love from our hearts to yours,

*Pat and Larry*

# We're All Connected in the Web of Life

*We are here to awaken*
*from our illusion of separateness.*
Thich Nhat Hanh

As I write this, the world is watching the daily unfolding of horrors in Ukraine, as the war continues. The massive destruction of cities and infrastructure is hard to watch, and our hearts go out to the millions of people who have lost their homes, their livelihood, and the necessities for survival.

As people flee in search of safety, I am heartened by the compassionate response of the citizens and governments of their neighboring countries. Equally uplifting is the response of people around the world. Modern technology enables us to witness events as they occur, and we are emotionally drawn in. Although we don't know them, we care about the Ukrainian people.

We feel connected to them. Love calls us to help, and we do what we can. Millions of people around the world are sending prayers and making financial contributions to organizations that are supporting people still in Ukraine and the refugees in other countries.

Once again, world events have focused our attention on our connection to one another. Sometimes it is easier to connect emotionally with people we don't know, who are clearly being victimized, than it is to feel connected to people we encounter personally whom we don't like for some reason.

Why is that? Larry and I have puzzled over this question.

Perhaps it is because, from a distance, we experience our shared humanity. Up close, we often lose sight of that and focus on the differences that we allow to divide us. Those differences get in the way of our kindness.

### Connecting in Person

We are at a time in history that requires us to put our ideas of separation aside and to remember our kinship with one another – not just with those who are like us, but with all others sharing the

Earth with us.

Our religions teach us to love one another. So, how did we get it so wrong through history and use our differences to hate and fear one another?

Religious ceremonies have been used for millennia to bring people together, to create a sense of community and belonging. The very experience of oneness that we feel when together in a familiar setting of a church, synagogue, mosque, temple – feeling the presence of a higher, loving power that protects us and guides our lives – the same experience has also been used to separate us from others who follow a different tradition.

In our religious traditions, we have ways of greeting one another with love and respect - Shalom (peace), Salaam (peace), Peace be with you, Namaste (I bow to you). These greetings carry a message of respect and honor that says, "I wish you well."

I was pleased to see the spirit of these ancient greetings show up in our modern culture. In the science fiction movie, Avatar, the indigenous people on a planet that had been invaded had a simple greeting for one another – "I see you." That rephrases all the religious greetings in a way that speaks to us today.

Do we really see each other - not just superficially, but in a deeper way, recognizing our inter-connection, our kinship? Or, as we encounter each other in our daily lives, do we see only the differences that separate us and trigger judgments that cause us to turn away rather than to reach out?

Have you ever been judged for something you said or something you did or for how you looked? Was there something inside of you calling out to be seen for all of who you are, not just the way you are showing up in this moment?

The way we see each other – those we know and those we are

just meeting – affects the way we respond to them. When we decide to live with kindness, we are choosing to stay in our hearts and not let our ego jump in with all of its judgments.

How different our response could be if we silently said, "I see you" to every person we meet. "I see you" puts us back in our hearts – it is calling on us to see beyond the way someone is expressing in this moment and to see the deeper truth of our essential connection.

### Can we do this?

We all have the power of choice. As you choose this as a silent mantra when you're out in the world, you will see no stranger, just family you have yet to meet. You may find that this is a way to expand your kindness journey - to open new opportunities for you to take your love out into the world.

As you read these words, no matter where you are, please know that we see you, and we appreciate your being in our life.

We're grateful that you are on this journey with us.

With love from our hearts to yours,

*Pat and Larry*

## Embrace Curiosity on Your Kindness Journey

*if you understand each other,*
*you will be kind to each other.*
John  Steinbeck

We all make judgments about others, based on attitudes we acquired from our families or from our own experiences. Over time, they become a part of us. When we withhold kindness from someone because of those judgments, we can be aware that we do not have enough information about them. We can choose to wonder about them.

Here is where I can call on my curiosity. I can open the door to connection by greeting someone I had ignored before with a smile and a nod, or a simple greeting. As I reach out in this way, I acknowledge the other person, and a connection is made. A short conversation may follow, and if I listen with an open mind and open heart, I will begin to see that we share certain experiences or hopes for our lives.

Of course, I don't need to get to know someone in order to drop my judgments. I can change the way I am looking at them. By looking through a kindness lens, I can see that each person is doing the best he or she can in this moment.

**Curiosity brings me back into my heart**

I could ask myself:

If I had been born into the life that she was born into, what would my childhood have been like and who would I be now? What economic opportunities and support systems did I have that he did not have? What mental or physical disabilities are contributing to her behavior now?

What natural talents was he born with that his life path did not enable him to develop, so he is not now enjoying the expression of those talents and being supported by them? Did she have anyone supporting and loving her as she grew up, or was she on her own, even as a child, to figure out how to survive in this world?

I don't know the answers to any of these questions, and the answers would help me to understand why he is showing up in the world now in the way that he is.

Those answers would open my heart and enable me to see him as another myself – another person wanting to be seen and accepted, wanting to be loved and to express love, wanting all his basic needs to be met so he could have the space in his life to become all that he is capable of.

When I am back in my heart, kindness flows easily.

Curiosity also invites change. It might even open the door for us to look at own lives:

When we make a conscious choice to live with kindness, we are called to look at people through a compassionate lens.

## Self-Reflection

Self-reflection can be uncomfortable, but it often helps us to understand ourselves better. We may ask why it is so hard to be kind to some people. By considering our feelings, we might gain insights that will enable us to soften our judgments and expand our kindness practice.

Often, we don't give ourselves the opportunity to get to know people we disagree with. We see them as those people who are against me.

The Sufi poet, Rumi, shed some light on this:

*Your task is not to seek for love, but merely to seek and find all the barriers within yourself that you have built against it.*

That calls for some self-reflection. I realize that so much of what shows up in our lives is a result of the lens through which we view others. As hard as it is for us to look at, we do have to admit that we build barriers to love when we see people who disagree with us as our enemies. That puts up a wall between them and us that prevents us from even trying to understand each other.

**Curiosity is an antidote to judgment.**

Many of us have allowed religious and political views to solidify into intractable positions of "I am right, and you are wrong, I am a good guy, and you are an enemy." As a country, we have turned the idea of brotherhood into one of "us and them."

How did we get to this ugly place once again?

I believe that we forgot how to love each other. Love does not mean agreeing on everything. It means working to understand each other and to find common ground on which to build a future together.

**Turn judgment into curiosity.**

Step one is to be curious. Why do they think that way? What do they really want for their lives? Can we find common ground and remember our kinship?

Paul Tillich answers these with a simple formula:

*The first duty of love is to listen.*

How do we even begin to answer these questions if we are not talking to each other?

**Daryl Davis**

The Black musician, Daryl Davis, provides an example. He has made it his mission to befriend people in hate groups like the Klu Klux Klan by calmly confronting them with the question: "How can you hate me if you don't even know me?"

"Give them a platform," he said. "You challenge them. But you don't challenge them rudely or violently. You do it politely and intelligently. And when you do things that way, chances are they will reciprocate and give you a platform."

That approach leads to the discovery of the common ground you both stand on - values, hopes for the future, what you really want for your lives. Once you find out that you agree on many issues, the barriers come down and you no longer see each other as enemies.

Daryl's efforts resulted in several clansmen becoming his friend and giving up their clan membership. Our challenge is a bit different, but the message is the same. When we take down the barriers in ourselves that prevent us from getting to know people who disagree with us, we find that we have more in common than we thought.

### We are more alike than we realize.

Of course, most of us do not have the time or inclination to go out and engage people one-on-one in conversation about our different views. But we can begin by accepting the idea that we do have a lot in common. We are all individuals, and we cannot be painted by the same brush, which is colored by the ideas in someone else's head about who we are.

### We have the power to change.

We do have the power to let go of judgments about each other and to remind ourselves that we are probably more alike than we thought. Then we will remember how to love each other and to begin to build a better future together.

Love is what the world needs now, and it's ours to give. Let's expand and deepen our kindness journey and flood the world with love, sweet love.

We're grateful that you are on this journey with us.

With love from our hearts to yours,

*Pat and Larry*

## Courage Empowers Our Kindness Journey

*Courage takes you out of your comfort zone
and into your power center.
Dr. Debra Reble*

Many people think that kindness is a wishy washy way of living. Quite the contrary, kindness is a powerful force for good in the world, and it becomes an even greater force when empowered by courage.

The word "courage" comes from the French word "oeur", which means "heart." By taking a step with courage, we connect with our power center and discover a strength within that we did not know we had.

Sometimes courage is required in order to just keep going during challenging times, not giving in to despair or the feeling that there is no good way out of this situation.

Often, kindness will help us to make that shift. Being kind does not mean standing down or not engaging on an important issue. It simply guides us to show up peacefully and to state our position in a way that does not demonize other people who hold a different point of view.

When we make a commitment to live with kindness, we open the door to opportunities that will invite us to expand our kindness practice. Eventually, we will encounter difficult situations that require us to step out of our comfort zone.

When we are reluctant to take that step, it's time for self-reflection.

### The courage to look at myself

*The chief danger in life is that you may take too many precautions.*

~ Alfred Adler

A starting point may be to ask, "From whom am I withholding kindness?" This will help me to look at the judgments I have about others and to consider how I can see them through a kinder lens.

Do I judge others based on appearance, behavior, ethnicity, religion, political party? Do those things determine my behavior toward them? If so, I am giving away the power to be in charge of my own behavior.

When I chose to live with kindness, I was choosing who I wanted to be in the world. I was choosing to see the humanity in others, to remember our kinship. From that perspective, I am able to drop my judgments and to respond to others with the assumption that they are doing the best they know how to do in this moment.

Then I am ready to take the next step.

### The courage to step out of my comfort zone

*Sometimes bravery is simply choosing to take the next step without fully knowing the path.*

Glennon Doyle

Most of us have kindness habits – certain circumstances in which we find it easy to be kind. When people see us coming, they smile, because they remember us, and we are comfortable being with them.

Sometimes, we are given the opportunity to be kind in situations that ask more of us. It might be as easy as a pleasant greeting, acknowledging someone we might have passed by previously. A brief conversation might follow, and that connection could uplift both of us.

### The Bystander Effect

At other times, we may witness someone in need of help, but that requires more of us than just a smile and a few pleasant words. Perhaps others see it also, but they choose to ignore it, not wanting to become involved.

When a situation calls for action, but no one else is helping, it is easier to be influenced by group thinking. Something inside of us knows that our response could make a difference, but we are reluctant to help. We can tell ourselves, "It is none of my business" or "Someone else could help, why should it be me?"

This is called "the bystander effect." It is an opportunity for us to take the lead and to be an example. When one person has the courage to respond with kindness, others will usually step up to help as well.

Once we have stepped out of our comfort zone a time or two, it becomes easier the next time we are given the opportunity. Our choice becomes more clear if we ask, "What would I want someone else to do if that were me or someone that I love needing help?"

A kind intervention can bring a positive outcome to a difficult situation. It uplifts us, the person we help, and anyone who witnesses our act of kindness. When people have witnessed someone else's kindness, they are more likely to intervene the next time they are called upon to help another person. There can be a ripple effect from one act of courage.

**The courage to take a stand on an issue I care about:**

*I raise up my voice–not so I can shout out,*
*but so that those without a voice can be heard...*

Malala Yousafzai

It takes courage to take a stand for what we see as right in the face of what we see as wrong. When we speak up in a family discussion with a point of view that is in opposition to the views of others, we risk being rejected.

When we speak out in public against a current injustice, we risk even more. Taking a stand often requires courage, especially if your message is speaking out against commonly accepted practices or what other people believe.

Sometimes taking a stand requires activism. In our culture today, we often think of activism as cultural and political protest, but it is much more. It can take the form of determined advocacy at various levels of government. It can be expressed through written or video messages to inform the public of an important issue. In some cases, it can be a dramatic single act to bring attention to a current or impending tragedy.

Behind every action of advocacy is a cause that people feel passionately about because it affects their lives or the lives of people they care about. It is an act of love.

Now, whenever I see or read about demonstrations for or against something, I ask myself, "Who or what do they love? What quality of life do they want more of or what are they fighting against that prevents them from having a missing quality in their lives – or in someone else's life?"

Advocacy means speaking out, but it can also mean joining an organization that is working to find solutions and to improve an issue that I care about. That might mean showing up to help with my hands and feet, ready to do the required work.

At any level, taking a stand requires courage, and in stepping up to the challenge, we often find power within that we did not know we had. In the process, we expand our kindness circle and help to create the world we choose to live in.

We're grateful that you are on this journey with us.

With love from our hearts to yours,

*Pat and Larry*

# Compassion is the heart of Kindness

*Love and compassion are necessities, not luxuries.*
*Without them humanity cannot survive.*
                                        - Dalai Lama

By choosing to live with kindness, we also invited compassion to accompany us on our journey. Compassion is concern for the sufferings or misfortunes of others, combined with a desire to help. It also has another dimension, which is usually ignored.

## It Begins with Self-Compassion

*If your compassion does not include yourself,*
*it is incomplete.*
… Buddha

Many of us carry within us regrets and even shame for things we have done in the past. We need to take time to accept our past, to forgive ourselves and to focus on living now in the best way we can.

This is the time to be kind to yourself. Set time aside every day to nurture yourself.

You might connect with a friend and have a little adventure or just a heart-to-heart conversation. Often friends see us through a more forgiving lens than we see ourselves, and they can give us the uplift that we need.

You may also be nourished by time to yourself. It might be quiet time with a cup of coffee or tea, writing in a journal, listening to your favorite music, lingering in a soothing bath or going for a walk. You might leave a favorite book by your bed to read at night or watch a TV show that makes you laugh.

A journal provides a way to reflect on your day and to make sense of all that happened. By recording your interactions with others, you have a way to acknowledge yourself for things that went well and to think about those that didn't. Then you can set an intention for tomorrow and ask your inner wisdom to guide you to a better approach next time. Think about activities that support you. Then be sure to incorporate some of them in your daily life.

## Treating Others with Compassion

*It's one of the hardest things in the world to be willing to empathize with a person in a moment when they seem not to deserve it the most.*

Megan Phelps-Roper

The way we view each other lays the foundation on which everything else is built. For most of us, it is normal to see some people as friends or family, some as strangers who seem like nice people. It is easy to share a smile or a kind word with them.

Other people who show up in our lives trigger a different response. We may quickly have thoughts of judgment, which make it more difficult to feel moved to kindness. As we expand our compassion, more and more, we show up as a channel for love in every encounter with others, no matter how they show up.

Living with Kindness means deciding to take the best part of us out into the world. As we expand how we express our kindness, more and more, we show up as a channel for love wherever we go, in every encounter with others, no matter how they are showing up.

It's easy and rewarding to expand our kindness journey by joining a local organization as a volunteer. One advantage of this step into service to those in need is the opportunity it offers us for our own personal growth. Often, we are asked to step out of our comfort zone and to expand our understanding of others less fortunate – perhaps some of whom we may have judged in the past.

Nobody has taken the concept of love-in-action to a higher level than Father Gregory Boyle, whose work with former gang members and ex-offenders has brought him world-wide acclaim.

He shares with us an expanded vision of a compassionate society:

*"Imagine a circle of compassion and imagine no one is standing outside that circle.*

*That is the goal and to that end, we stand with the people who suffer,*

*with the poor and the powerless, the voiceless.*

*And to that end, we stand with the people whose dignity has been denied*

and we stand with those whose burdens are more than they can bear.

*And when you're really lucky, you get to stand with the easily despised and the readily left out.*

*You get to stand with the demonized, so the demonizing will stop,*

*and with the disposable, so the day will come when we stop throwing people away."*

As a pastor in the poorest Catholic parish, with the highest concentration of gang activity in Los Angeles, Father Boyle sought a compassionate and effective approach to gang members. He eventually left his parish duties and helped found Homeboy Industries, which became the largest gang intervention, rehabilitation, and re-entry program in the world.

This not-for-profit organization serves high risk men and women by offering hope, training and job skills, with the goal of helping them to redirect their lives and become contributing members of their families and their community.

By serving some of the most demonized people in our society, Father Boyle and his staff and volunteers show us the rewards of taking loving kindness into places that had been written off as untouchable. They created a truly safe and loving place where lives are transformed – the lives of those who are served and those who serve them, as well.

*"All of us are called to go the very edges of the circle of compassion,*

*with sure and certain hope that if you stand there, the circle will widen,*

*and people who are outside will be let in."*

That is an invitation to all of us to expand our own circle of compassion. When we do, we will be transformed in the process.

But we each get to choose the path that is right for us at this moment in our lives. Every act of kindness makes a difference in the world. You are in charge of deciding how you share your love with others.

No matter how you do it, you are a force for good and you do make a difference in the world.

*Compassion is even more powerful than courage. Sure, with courage*

*you can conquer the world, but only with compassion,*

*you can heal and build it.*

Rasheed Ogunlaru

**Together, We Are Building a Kinder World**

Most people underestimate the power we all have to influence the direction of our community, our country, and even our world. We are interconnected in ways we have never seen before.

Community has now become, not just a neighborhood, but a country-wide or world-wide gathering of people who come together electronically to explore a shared interest or even work together on a shared mission. With the benefits of video gatherings, we can see each other and interact in a more meaningful way.

We are also able to hear what others are doing to address problems that we are facing in our lives or our country. We learn from each other across physical boundaries, as we find that we are not separate, but one extended human family with a lot to share with each other.

As I write this, we are now all witnessing the unfolding upheaval of people's lives in Ukraine. We are also seeing an outpouring of compassion and constructive support from people of many countries. The world seems to have come together, despite differences that we might have, in support of people we do not know.

We are experiencing our kinship.

Gregory Boyle said that his work arose from two questions that he lived with:

*"There's an idea that's taken root in the world ...*
*that there just might be lives out there that matter less than*
*other lives.*
*How do we stand against that idea?"*
*"How do we achieve a compassion that allows us to stand in*
*awe of what others have to carry*
*rather than stand in judgment of how they carry it?"*

Perhaps considering these questions could illuminate all our lives.

We're grateful that you are on this journey with us.

With love from our hearts to yours,

*Pat and Larry*

# Creating a Worldwide Kindness Community

*There are no strangers here,*
*only friends you haven't yet met*
... William Butler Yeats

We are communal beings. We have an instinct to come together, but our culture has created economic and social conditions that separate us from one another. Many people feel isolated and cut off from others.

Kindness creates a bridge between us.

Living with Kindness is one of hundreds of communities around the world that bring together people who want to use their lives to help create a kinder world. In the previous post, *Changing to a Culture of Kindness*, we shared information about four organizations with large followings that are having an impact on the world. They are a tiny piece of the total picture of change happening in our global culture.

All over the world, people wanting to live together peacefully are coming together and inspiring others with their example. Many are actively spreading the messages of love and kindness, creating virtual communities. At Living with Kindness, we eagerly join with the millions of people who are demonstrating the power of love with their lives.

The mission of the Living with Kindness Community is to provide a safe place where we are free to express who we truly are, to talk about our kindness journey, to inspire and support each other in finding ways to expand our kindness practice.

In our community, inspiration comes from all of us. We are each on a unique journey, and by sharing our experiences and what we learn from them, we find that we all have gems of wisdom to share with one another.

### Building Community

*Alone we can do so little. Together we can do so much.*

Helen Keller

We build community when we join with others who are on a

similar kindness path, as we inspire each other with our stories and our wisdom.

Community also enables us to take our kindness practice to the next level – to receive encouragement and support to act with love in unfamiliar encounters. That part of our journey has unexpected rewards, as we discover the gifts that the people whom we had previously ignored have to offer us, enriching our lives as we enrich theirs.

We all contribute to the unfolding history of our country and our world. Let's use our part in that emerging story to come together and to add more love and kindness where it is so desperately needed. We cannot change the whole world, but we have the power to change our lives and those of people we meet.

If you are living with kindness, you are already making a difference in the world in your daily life. If you wish to receive inspiration and share ideas with others on a similar path, we invite you to join us. As we come together, we truly become a powerful force for good in the world.

Welcome to the Living with Kindness community.

We're grateful that you are on this journey with us.

With love from our hearts to yours,

*Pat and Larry*

## Living with Kindness Makes Life a Celebration

*One should never, but never,*
*pass by an opportunity to celebrate.*
— j d malouf

Life offers us so many opportunities to celebrate. We usually think of celebrating special moments in our life journey - anniversaries, birthdays, major accomplishments.

At these times, we stop and enjoy the moment. Sharing with others – the exchange of love and appreciation - enriches the occasion. It might take the form of a party or an evening out with friends or family.

A celebration is a chance to let go of whatever stress we might carry about on-going obligations or thoughts we have about what we need to do next. It is a time-out from daily concerns. It is a time to refresh and experience joy.

That is good for us. So, how do we get more of it in our lives?

We begin by expanding our ideas about celebration – finding ways to celebrate life every day, no matter what our circumstances might be.

### Little celebrations

*Each day offers a reason to celebrate.*

Amy Leigh Mercree

Look for something every day to celebrate. When we create a habit to notice what is around us, wherever we go, we allow ourselves to enjoy the little details in our lives.

We see a flower in our neighbor's yard or in a planter in front of a store. We stop, take in the colors, the fragrance, and the symmetry of the petals. We let the wonder of it fill us and we enjoy the moment of appreciation for what life just offered us.

Enjoying that moment is a celebration of the beauty in our lives. A quiet moment of appreciation. We feel uplifted and the day seems brighter.

In our homes, we have many things that give us pleasure – items that we have chosen because they gave us joy, and we wanted them to be part of our life. Items that others gave us that carry special meaning because of our relationship.

Do we stop and notice and appreciate them, or have they become just a part of the backdrop of our lives? When we take a few minutes to enjoy the beauty of an item or the sweetness of the memory it triggers, we celebrate the moment with gratitude – for the beauty or for the sweet memory it brings.

It is a small celebration of our life.

We have daily opportunities to celebrate life. Every time we encounter someone and greet them with a smile and a kind word, we are adding joy to our life and to theirs. We also have an opportunity to expand our moments of celebration to a way of being in the world.

### Celebration becomes a way to live life

*Life is a Festival of celebration.*

Anthony T. Hincks

Life becomes a celebration when we live with kindness. By looking for ways to acknowledge and uplift others, we experience the joy that comes from that connection. The people we greet experience the joy of receiving our kindness.

That joy is contagious. Happy people are more likely to be kind, and they will pass it on to others. It becomes an ever-expanding circle of kindness.

Many people already have daily rituals – prayer or meditation, writing in a journal, playing music, walking in the neighborhood or in a park. These help us to connect to ourselves in a deeper way. They are quiet ways to celebrate life.

We can expand the role that rituals play in our lives by transforming some of our daily habits, giving them special meaning that they did not have before.

Our favorite ritual is our morning coffee-and-tea-time, when we share with one another our dreams and memories, music, poetry or articles that uplifted us, ideas and inspirations that are guiding our current projects. They are special times together that include gratitude and appreciation for each other and for our life.

We can transform any chore into a ritual by imbuing it with appreciation and gratitude. Providing care for a loved one becomes more than an obligation. It becomes a special time to connect with each other. Preparing food can be a time to feel appreciation for the abundance in our lives and for the people who enjoy the meals we prepare. Even house cleaning can be a time to be grateful for our home.

When we are with family, friends or co-workers, we can see it as a celebration of our life together, as we think about the gifts that we each bring – even those that challenge each other. We can be grateful for the personal growth that comes from living together, as well as the joy that our relationships bring.

Our life becomes a celebration when we live with an open heart and look at it through a lens of gratitude and love.

We wish you joy as you discover new ways to celebrate your life.

We're grateful that you are on this journey with us.

With love from our hearts to yours,

*Pat and Larry*

## How Do We Bring Light into a World of Conflict?

*Act as if what you do makes a difference.*
*It does.*
~ William James

As we participate in the emotional ups and downs of political reality in our country and observe the chaotic and sometimes horrific challenges that other people are facing around the world, we find ourselves in turbulent waters, swirling with hate, fear, anger, sadness, despair, hope, compassion, and inspired determination.

In the past week, Larry and I found ourselves overwhelmed with sadness, and yes, some anger, as we witnessed what seemed to be the country we love falling apart in slow motion. It was hard. We allowed ourselves to be with those feelings, to express them to each other, and then to take time to work through the process of returning to the balance we needed to move forward.

We wondered how we could find a way to inject love and kindness into the mix, when the mix has become so toxic. As we talked about how, if at all, we could help to heal our country, we realized that now, more than ever, messages of kindness are needed.

We remember the song, *What the World Needs Now Is Love, Sweet Love*. That is like a clarion call to all of us.

We have made the choice to live with kindness, and that was not conditional, based on what other people were doing. It was a commitment to ourselves not to allow what is going on in the world to distract us from spreading love in whatever way we can.

Every act of kindness is love in action. It has a positive impact on the people receiving the kindness and those observing it. It often has a ripple effect, as others are inspired to pass it on. By continuing daily acts of kindness, we do make a difference in our world.

Often, kindness calls on us to take a stand for what we believe is right. For many people, the way forward is taking action in the political arena. That can be done in a way that contributes to healing, if it is done, not with hatred of those who disagree with us, but with a focus on creating the more positive outcome that we want.

As we participate in any action, we need to be mindful of the energy with which we engage in the struggle. We can let anger motivate us to take action, but we need to act in a way that brings reason and compassion into the mix.

We need to find a way to live together peacefully if we are to survive as a country and as a world.

We do not have all the answers to a kinder world. We don't even have most of them. Our intention is always to offer ideas, without judging whether anyone accepts the invitation to experiment in their own lives with the ideas we share.

Now, even more than before, we want your input. We all have wisdom from our life experiences, and we all benefit when others share what has helped them to get through difficult times.

Thank you for joining us on this journey.

We're grateful that you are on this journey with us.

With love from our hearts to yours,

*Pat and Larry*

# The Kindness Impulse – An Uplifting Story

*There are no strangers here*
*Just friends you haven't yet met.*
… William Butler Yeats

We are born with an innate tendency to connect with others. Larry calls it the kindness impulse.

In our culture today, many people feel disconnected from each other, even at work and in their apartment building or neighborhood.

Most of us are able to create connections – through work, school, or places of worship or through shared interests. Now, we can also connect online with people we would not be likely to meet otherwise. That has opened a door to a virtual community.

Today we celebrate the online platform Nextdoor, which enables people to reach out to strangers, in a neighborhood and beyond, to share information, to ask for suggestions on finding what they need, to ask for help with a problem or to offer help.

I recently turned to Nextdoor to help our friend, Laura. I posted this request for help:

"Do you have a bicycle that you are not using?

Our friend, Laura, is living on the street. She recently lost her bicycle, which she depended on to get her to the services and counseling that help her, not only to survive, but to get her life turned around. Her bike had two baskets behind the seat, straddling the back wheel, which enabled her to carry her sleeping bag and other belongings with her. Her bike also had excellent speed.

Laura is a kind, gentle woman who has experienced serious challenges in her life. If you have or know of someone who has a bicycle that could help her navigate the obstacles in her daily life, please contact me. Thank you for your kindness."

Posting a request on Nextdoor is opening a door for people to help, and two strangers felt the kindness impulse.

Matt replied, "I might have one, how tall is she?" and Amy

wrote, "Lemme know if I can help! Rack? Basket? Bike lock? Water cages & bottles."

It turned out that Matt has a bicycle and motorcycle maintenance and repair business, and he happened to have just the right bike for Laura. He also had the baskets that Laura needed. He put in the time to refurbish the bike, and Amy contacted him and covered his out-of-pocket expenses.

The highlight of my week was being present when Laura took her new bike for a trial run. There were some tears of joy.

Now, if we ever want help, for ourselves or for someone else, we know to turn to Nextdoor first. We encourage you to do the same or find another online platform that connects people. Our community really is larger than we realized – and so is yours.

We believe that we all have a kindness impulse within us. It enriches our lives when we follow its calling.

We're grateful that you are on this journey with us.

With love from our hearts to yours,

*Pat and Larry*

## Small Acts of Kindness Make a Big Difference

*The best portion of a good man's life*
*is his little, nameless, unremembered*
*acts of kindness and of love.*
~ William Wordsworth

As we go through our day, we often have opportunities to be kind. Some require very little of us – a smile or a pleasant word. Others ask more from us, but they are still easy, within our comfort zone. We may assume that because they are small, they don't make much of a difference, but that is not necessarily true.

There are no insignificant acts of kindness, no matter how small they may seem to be.

There are different ways of thinking about the impact of kindness:

## The Ripple Effect

Every act of kindness has an energy that goes out beyond the people involved. Some people call it the ripple effect. The person receiving the kindness may have her mood uplifted and begin to be kinder to others. People observing the kindness may be inspired to look for opportunities to do the same.

We never know the extent of the ripple, but we do know that as others pass kindness on in their lives, that will create new ripples, and the impact of the original act is multiplied many times over.

## The Kindness Boomerang

Orly Wahba, founder of Life Vest Inside, has devoted her life to spreading messages of kindness and teaching young people the joy of being kind. Her video, *The Kindness Boomerang*, went viral, carrying the message that the kindness we give, not only spreads, but eventually returns to us, making its rounds through the lives of others on its way back to us.

We have noticed in our own lives and by observing other people's lives, that the kinder we are, the more often kind people show up in our lives. We don't see it as a direct line from one act through others back to us. We see it as an energy that we put out and it returns to us in kind.

## We call this The Circle of Kindness.

It is not linear. There is usually no direct connection between our actions and the way in which kindness comes back to us. But we are sure that the energy we put out eventually returns, and it can come in the most surprising ways, often just as we need it most

Sometimes, I can see – or imagine - a connection. One memory always comes to mind.

When my daughter, Christie, was a teenager, she and I had spent a few days in New York City as tourists from Arizona. Then, I put her on a train in Pennsylvania Station so she could spend a few weeks with her best friend, Christine, who was staying for the summer with her grandmother in Pennsylvania. It was Christie's first trip on her own.

I traveled uptown to Grand Central Station, where I was going to take a train to Connecticut to spend time with my mother. As I walked toward my gate, I was approached by a young man who asked me if I had $5 so he could get a train ticket home. Without stopping to consider if he was being honest or just panhandling, I said "Of course" and gave him $5. If that had been Christie, what would I want someone to do for her?

Later that evening, Christie called my mother's phone – it was long before cell phones – and told me her story. She had missed her stop and panicked when she realized it. The woman sitting next to her on the train assured her that it would be alright. She was getting off at the next stop and offered to drive Christie back to the right station. They easily connected with Christine and her grandmother.

We all learned something about kindness that day. Not so

much about the mechanics of it, but about how we can count on it to show up – for kind people to show up – when we are most in need.

In the circle of kindness, we are all in the flow of giving and receiving. We don't have to understand how it works. Just knowing that it does empowers us to make choices that keep us in the flow.

Kindness becomes a way of life.

We're grateful that you are on this journey with us.

With love from our hearts to yours,

*Pat and Larry*

# The Pause that Refreshes

*When we pause, allow a gap and breathe deeply,*
*we can experience instant refreshment.*
... Pema Chödrön

As we walk our kindness path, most days go smoothly, as we easily engage people with pleasant comments, and they usually respond in kind. Some days, however, lead us to more challenging situations that trigger a habitual reaction in us – one of annoyance or anger.

Most of us are still experiencing these little bumps in the road. When we get to the point where we are ready to move beyond reaction, we need to look at what triggers us and find a way to shift our response.

This takes some pre-paving, preparing us for the next encounter. First, we need to understand that we have more power over our response than we realize.

**The power is in the pause.**

Typically, when someone triggers us, we think that the next step is our reaction to it. Actually, there is a space between the stimulus and the response. Most do not realize that, so we don't take advantage of it.

The incident triggers our interpretation of what it means, and then, we are reacting to the meaning that we have given it. In the space between, we can shift the meaning and therefore, be able to respond in a more positive way.

How do we do that?

First, decide not to react. Give yourself time to reframe the situation in your mind.

Then, change your thinking. Replace the meaning you have given the incident with a more positive thought that gives the other person space to show up in the way that he is in this moment.

As you think about your last encounter, you might practice a new way of seeing the other person in a kinder light:

"He's having a bad day. I don't need to add to it."

"I don't know what's going on with him, but it's about him, not me"

"My response is about me, not him."

Then, your response might be as simple as ignoring whatever the other person said that triggered you. It might be a brief answer such as "I hear you" or some other neutral comment that does not lead to confrontation.

When we ask, "Who do I want to be in this moment?" we bring our focus back on ourselves, and that helps us to get more clarity about how to proceed.

This all takes some practice, especially if we have a strong habit of reaction. If you find it difficult to remember your newly chosen response, it's ok to say, "Excuse me, I'm taking a few minutes, but I'll be back," then walk away.

In these situations, your power is in the pause, the space for you to reframe the incident to one that is manageable.

As you master the art of the pause, you take a giant step forward on your kindness path.

And isn't that refreshing?

We're grateful that you are on this journey with us.

With love from our hearts to yours,

*Pat and Larry*

## Let's Help Our Children To Be Kind

*Nothing can make our life, or the lives of other people,*
*more beautiful than perpetual kindness.*
Leo Tolstoy

The most important thing we need to do for our children and grandchildren is to provide a place where they feel safe and loved. Everything else we do is to help create that experience for them. Our job is to support and reinforce their natural inclination to be kind.

**Our Children are Naturally Loving and Compassionate**

My observations, and those of many other parents, support the idea that our children are not just self-centered and insensitive. They are capable of sensitivity and compassion.

When my daughter, Christie, was just a toddler and her vocabulary was still quite limited, on two different occasions, she showed me that she was able to relate to the feelings of others and to respond with empathy.

**The first involved the book "Peter Rabbit."**

I had read it to her more than once so, even though she could not verbalize it, she knew the story. I was in the kitchen, and she was in the living room looking through the book.

All of a sudden, I realized that she was crying. I went to her to see what was wrong.

There on her lap, the book was opened to the page that showed Peter Rabbit trapped inside Mr. McGregor's garden. Peter was crying. And Christie was crying with him.

She had never cried when I read her the story, but there she was, sitting alone with Peter Rabbit before her. She reached out to him in her imagination, and he touched her heart.

I comforted her and reminded her that Peter did get out of the garden and go home to his mother. I found the picture of Peter with his mother at the end of the story. Then she looked up at me and smiled.

This was not a self-centered child. She was fully engaged

with Peter Rabbit, and she responded with compassion.

I was taken aback. From that moment on, I realized that there was a lot more going on within her than I could even imagine.

**The second incident was even more astonishing to me.**

Christie was about two. I was pregnant with my son, David, and very happy at the thought of having another child.

But one day, as happens with pregnant women, I was feeling sad - for no apparent reason. I was lying on the couch on my side, watching Christie play on the carpet near me.

All of a sudden, she looked at me, stood up and walked over to the couch. Then she did one of the most tender, loving things anyone has ever done for me. She put her cheek down on my cheek and held it there for several seconds.

It was a gesture of such love and compassion that it brought tears to my eyes.

All of our children have such wonderful gifts to share with us. How do we create a safe, loving environment that will support them and enable them to grow into emotionally healthy adults?

### Creating a Kind Family

Of course, we want them to grow up being kind. We do that by modeling kindness in our interactions with them, considering what we can do to help them to feel safe, welcomed and appreciated.

### Express appreciation.

"Thank you" is a way to say that you appreciate something kind that your child did. The message is strengthened by a specific response that acknowledges your child's thoughtfulness, such as "I love these flowers" in response to a handful of dandelions picked in the yard.

The more we thank them, the more children find ways to be

kind.

As they get older and contribute to household chores, we often forget to acknowledge their contributions. It means a lot to hear words of appreciation for what they do to keep the household running.

**Give them opportunities to contribute.**

Young children are naturally helpful. They want to be a part of what we are doing, and they feel good when they help.

I had always encouraged my son and daughter to help at home. Christie was in fifth grade and David was in second grade when the three of us were on our own, and then it became more important that they help around the house.

That time of transition gave me an opportunity to upgrade our relationship. We became a team.

**Give them a voice in decision-making.**

I wanted them to feel that their ideas mattered, so I began having weekly family meetings. It gave me a chance to check in with them and for them to have a say in family matters. We talked about what was going well and where they needed help. We planned our weekend activities together.

At first, I expected them to keep their rooms neat and to help with light chores. As they got older, we decided together how to keep the household running smoothly.

I made a list of all the chores that needed to be done daily and weekly. Christie offered to take notes. Then we discussed how to assign chores. Christie liked indoor activities and David liked yard work, so that part was easy.

They came up with the idea of placing a difficulty rating on each chore based on how long it took, how difficult it was, and, also, the "yuckiness factor." You can imagine that cleaning the bathroom was yucky. David said that trimming back the hedge of pyracantha bushes along the wall in the backyard also qualified, because they we full of long, sharp thorns.

It took a while to rate all the chores and to distribute them in as fair a way as possible. Of course, I had mine, too. We agreed to rotate between us those that no one wanted.

I monitored how well everything got done, and we revisited the schedule during our weekly meetings, making adjustments as needed.

We also decided on house rules together:

- to talk politely to each other and not to raise our voices in the house.
- to do homework and chores before play.
- to be home by curfew – the times changed as they got older.
- to call if we were going to be late.
- Consequences if we broke a rule - they decided those themselves.

All the rules applied to me, also. One evening I was late coming home because I had an evening presentation as part of my job, and I had forgotten to call Christie. She had already prepared supper for her and David, but this was before cell phones, so she had no idea what happened to me.

When I walked in two hours late, she stood with her hands on her hips and told me, "You're grounded." I laughed and agreed, and I did not go out that weekend. Fairness is also a part of kindness.

As I look back on my parenting years, I remember the challenges, but mostly, I remember the joy of the journey that I shared with two kind and wise young people who helped me to become who I am today.

Wherever you are on your journey, we wish you love and joy. We're grateful that you are on this journey with us.

With love from our hearts to yours,

*Pat and Larry*

## What Would Happen if Schools Taught Kindness?

*What would education look like if its purpose were not
to create a workforce, but whole human beings?*
Parker Palmer

Andy Smallman is a teacher who wrote his master's thesis on "trying to empower children to take charge of their education." He believed that allowing them to pursue their interests and to follow their curiosity, they would remain engaged and be excited about learning.

He wondered what would happen if a school included kindness in its curriculum. As part of a group of parents who started the Puget Sound Community School (PSCS) in 1994, he had an opportunity to find out. The school, for grades 6 to 12, was "founded upon the belief that people are intrinsically compelled by their own curiosity and desires to learn, and when provided a positive and supportive environment ...will enthusiastically pursue meaningful and challenging tasks."

Andy created a program that enabled students to experience the pleasure that comes from acts of kindness. The program was designed to take people on a journey, learning different ways to expand the reach of their kindness as they perform the recommended actions in the program.

The experiment with the students in their school was so successful that, in 2011, Andy created an online version of the program open to the public. 250 "students" from around the world practiced random acts of kindness that had a positive impact on their communities.

The website, *Kind Living*, invites anyone of any age to experience the kindness practices in the program. *Kind Living* promotes ordinary activities that "awaken kindness and awe, helping people connect to their true nature and increase peace in the world."

The program consists of 5 modules. Each module includes three assignments, so anyone completing the entire course will have performed at least 15 different types of kind acts. Andy recommends taking a week for each type, doing at least one kind act every day.

**Module 1 - Practice of Kindness**

Do something kind for yourself.

Do something kind for a good friend (or family member)

Do something kind for a stranger

**Module 2 - Anonymous Kindness**

Do something small.

Provide something wonderful for someone to find

Enlist a partner

**Module 3 - Twilight Zone Kindness** - using a classic tv show to inspire acts of kindness.

**Module 4 - Stargirl Kindness** - The novel of a fictional teenage girl inspired kindness.

**Module 5 - Did I Ever Tell You How Lucky You Are?** - Kindness inspired by the delightful book by Dr. Seuss.

## Creating Ripples

Andy summed up his inspiration for the program: "It was the idea of throwing a little pebble into a pond and seeing how far the ripples would go," he said. "If more people realize what they do with their acts of kindness ... we will live in a better place."

What would our world be like if all schools provided opportunities for children to discover the joy that comes from practicing kindness?

We're grateful that you are on this journey with us.

With love from our hearts to yours,

*Pat and Larry*

# Invite Awe and Wonder into Your Daily Life

*Every moment is unique, offering its own way
to connect to what is deepest within us,
to the wonder and mystery of being fully alive.*
Llewellyn Vaughan-Lee

It is so easy to get caught up in the activity and demands of our daily lives that we don't take the time to reconnect with the beauty and wonder of the world around us and right in front of us.

So, how do we do that?

I remember a day, decades ago, when my daughter, Christie, was a baby in a stroller. As we traveled through our neighborhood, she noticed a flower growing near the road. Her face lit up as she pointed to it, with delight and wonder on her face. It was exquisite, and I bent down so I could enjoy the moment with her. As I took in the gift that the flower offered us, I also delighted in Christie's response to the beauty before her.

At that moment, I realized that I had passed that flower on my early morning walk, but had not noticed it, too absorbed in my thoughts about the day ahead.

Wonder comes naturally when we are present to the world around us. No matter what is happening in our lives, there is always so much to inspire awe and wonder. We just need to pay attention, rather than navigating our lives to get somewhere else, with our minds full of plans or worries or memories that prevent us from noticing what is around us.

This is easy when we're out in nature, away from our usual routines with deadlines and responsibilities. Walking through a forest or along a beach takes us out of ourselves and into the elegance of the living, thriving world. We are pulled out of our minds to the experience of being present with the majesty of a waterfall or the view from a mountain top.

Nature offers us tiny wonders as well. Wildflowers of many hues and shapes and sizes. The songs of birds and flashing colors as they fly past. Insects moving with purpose, on their own deliberate journey. The play of light as it dances around us. The music of flowing water and leaves rustling in a breeze. There are endless gifts that pull us out of our minds and awaken us to the wonder of our world.

But we don't have to get away from where we live to be in awe of the beauty of our world and the wonder of being alive in it. We can begin with noticing what a miracle it is that we are here, with eyes to see and ears to hear and noses to take in the fragrances that drift to us as we go through our day – and bodies that take us out into this amazing world, so we can experience the wonders it offers us.

Nature is right here as well. Flowers blooming in our yard or in a pot on our windowsill. The magic of a spider's intricate web that sparkles with dew in the early morning light. Birds gathering at a bird feeder to delight us as they revel in the bounty.

Just looking around as we move through our day, we can see beauty that we usually ignore or take for granted. People moving around us, each with a single purpose, but together, creating a dance of life. The movement of light and shadow as the day passes. Sounds of laughter and eager conversation, as people enjoy connecting and sharing time together.

We so easily get caught up in our daily routine that we forget to take time for wonder. Let's treat ourselves to the joy of noticing what an amazing world we live in. Videographer Louie Schwartzberg says, "When you experience wonder, your whole mind and body is arrested by something larger than yourself. You become what you behold…You're left with increased feelings of wellbeing, compassion and creativity… we become more patient, more willing to help other people."

Louie also highlights the purpose of beauty in nature. Flowers attract the pollinators who spread the pollen that ensures the continuation of the life of that species, and they provide the nourishment for the pollinators, ensuring their continuation, as well.

I encourage you to watch his TED Talk and to be in awe of the beauty of nature unfolding with the magic of his videography *Nature's Beauty Inspires Gratitude: Louie Schwartzberg at TEDxSMU.*

As you go through this week, we invite you to be open to the beauty around you and to experience the wonder of being alive in this amazing world. Then, notice the gratitude that wells up within you.

We're grateful that you are on this journey with us.

With love from our hearts to yours,

*Pat and Larry*

## Let's Be Better Humans

*When you get lost in the service of helping others,*
*it's a good place to get lost.*
Jon Linton

After the death of a friend who had become homeless due to an addiction, Jon Linton wanted to do something to help the homeless in Phoenix, Arizona. He began to take photographs of people living on the street to document their plight, and he volunteered at a local shelter.

When he introduced himself to a man who had given him permission to take his photo, Jon asked his name. The man wept, and he said, "You have no idea how long it has been since someone cared to ask my name."

That was the beginning of Jon's "I Have a Name project." He wanted to restore dignity, compassion and understanding for those who were often treated as if they did not exist. When we know a person's name, we acknowledge their humanity. We see them as more than an anonymous face in a sea of faces that we try not to look at because the reality of their lives is too difficult for us to respond to.

"When you look around here, you get a real sense of suffering," Jon said. "It's an indictment against a first world country when we allow elderly women to call the streets home."

With a passion to increase public awareness of the human tragedy of the lives of homeless people, Jon created an extensive exhibit of his photographic portraits of people living on the streets of Phoenix, along with the stories that some of his subjects chose to share. He believed that, if he could show people their humanity, more people would be inspired to volunteer with services that provide support for them and to advocate for policies that would help to get them into homes.

After taking his exhibit to several cities across The United States, Jon wanted to expand his service. In 2014, he founded

"Let's Be Better Humans," a non-profit organization that "directly supports the return of dignity to those in need."

"We all strive for purpose and understanding, to hear and to be heard, to see and to be seen, to leave this world a better place than we found it," Jon says.

Let's Be Better Humans is a reminder that "we exist for one another, that we can make a difference. In short, we are a revolution in love and humanity."

That vision inspired folks at The Southwest Institute of Healing Arts, and they provided funding for what Jon called "the Magic Bus." The bus enabled him to deliver food, water, clothing, and other essential items to the less fortunate in Arizona and California and other parts of the western United States.

Jon's expanded vision included other groups of people that he saw being treated as less than human. He participated in peaceful actions against deportation, bigotry and isolationism, and he joined in supporting "our friends from Planned Parenthood, the LGBTQ, Native American, Muslim and communities from every race, creed and color."

He believed that it was necessary to embrace the ideals of bridges over walls in his efforts to give a voice to "the downtrodden and the silenced."

Jon's vision found another outlet in 2016. Wayne Rainey, owner of MonOrchid art gallery in Phoenix's Roosevelt Row Arts District, wanted a large mural on an outside wall of his gallery. He collaborated with Jon and Phoenix artist Brian Boner to create "The Garden," in honor of people who have died on the streets, "often unnoticed and unacknowledged."

A red-headed boy is tipping a watering can from which hundreds of black birds spill out and fly onto the white wall of the building. The boy is standing on top of these words from Mother Teresa:

*"At the end of life, we will not be judged by how many diplomas we have received, how much money we have made, how many great things we have done.*

*We will be judged by "I was hungry, and you gave me something to eat, I was naked, and you clothed me. I was homeless, and you took me in."*

At the side of the mural is a plaque,

*"In honor and remembrance of those who have perished homeless on our streets."*

"To me," Jon said, "the birds represent freedom from poverty and oppression for the homeless. They're emblematic of those who have perished from it and are now in flight to a better place."

Brian Boner said that the boy spreads "a message of tolerance, compassion and humanity to the masses." It also serves to create dialogue about the unresolved issue of homelessness.

Kindness does not require anything more from us, but it does invite us to find ways that we can be of service to people who are less fortunate than we are. We have been inspired by many of our friends on the street, and we believe that you will also discover that, as you reach out with love, you will find new, unexpected friends.

Let's consider the invitation to be better humans, in whatever way that is right for us. We'll be glad that we did.

We're grateful that you are on this journey with us.

With love from our hearts to yours,

*Pat and Larry*

## The Gift of Listening to Each Other

Being heard is so close to being loved that,
for the average person, they are almost indistinguishable.
David W. Augsburger

If there were an easy way to expand the reach of your kindness in the world, would you want to use it?

Listening is a skill that we all use, but most of us need a little guidance on how to do it better. We're good at listening for information that we need, such as directions to a destination or instructions on how to do something that we need to do. But listening to someone else, to allow them to say what they need to say, takes listening to another level.

As a psychotherapist, Traci Ruble realized that many people in our society feel disconnected from others. They need to feel connected – not fixed or healed but accepted as they are.

In order to provide a way for that connection to happen, Traci and a colleague developed an experiment to create spaces of connection and belonging - on city sidewalks. They recruited others willing to join them, and on May 7, 2015, twenty-eight "listeners" took to the streets of San Francisco. Many of them had to get out of their comfort zones in order to put a chair on a sidewalk with a sign that says, "We're here to listen."

That day was so successful that they founded Sidewalk Talk, a community project that creates public spaces where people can connect and find a sense of belonging. Traci says "Sitting out on the street is a radically different kind of listening. It requires a deeper listening and a relational kind of presence."

The mission at Sidewalk Talk is "to inspire, teach, and practice heart-centered listening to create belonging, justice, and social health." Listening helps people to open up, to share more, and to connect in an increasingly lonely world.

The project has expanded to 50 cities in 12 countries. Each chapter offers the same invitation, "Hi. Would you like to be listened to?" Listeners return to the same public spaces, week after week "to renew our sense of belonging and connection and stem the growing tide of loneliness."

Sidewalk Talk is a grass-roots effort built by people in their local communities who wanted to be a part of a global movement. They are creating ongoing communities of listeners, who are trained to listen as equals and equipped with skills to intervene in a crisis. Their contribution to their communities is beyond measure. Judging from the people who return to share more, they are having a positive impact.

Most of us are not able or inclined to participate in this kind of a listening project, but we can benefit from simple ideas to improve our own listening skills.

First, we need to ask ourselves why we are listening to someone else. Is it:

- Listening to understand or
- Listening to wait for our turn to respond?

Our intention determines the degree of our attention to what is being said. It also determines the sincerity of our engagement in the conversation.

Conversation can help us to understand each other and to connect in a deeper way. Here are a few ideas that might improve the quality of that connection:

- Give your full attention to what the other person is saying.
- Make eye contact and have supportive body language – arms open not crossed, lean toward them, with an interested facial expression.
- Ask open-ended questions to show your interest and to deepen the connection.

- Let them finish speaking before asking a question, be patient if they need time to gather their thoughts.
- Empathetically repeat back to them the essence of what they said to affirm that you heard them correctly.
- Remember the details and write them down later for possible follow-up conversations.

As a good listener, it is important to make the conversation about them. Avoid the temptation to make it about you. Let your curiosity and a compassionate heart fuel your genuine interest in them. That will provide a safe place for them to be more open with you.

If we all learn to be better listeners, we will build a society that creates better mental health. As Traci Ruble said,

*I want us to imagine together that we create a better world where everybody belongs.*

*Where everybody that needs to be heard, has a story to tell, knows that there's a listener on the other end of that story.*

*And I want you to imagine what problems we would solve if we actually created that.*

Let's see what we can do to help bring that world into being.

We're grateful that you are on this journey with us.

With love from our hearts to yours,

*Pat and Larry*

## Seeing Others Through a Kindness Lens

*The true greatness of a person is evident in the way he or she treats those with whom courtesy and kindness are not required.*
~ Joseph B. Wirthlin

Most people are kind, but circumstances often determine when and where we express our kindness.

**Someone is rude to me.**

It is natural for us to respond to other people in the way that they have treated us.

If someone is rude, we respond in kind, almost as an instinct to protect ourselves. We are not reacting to dangerous animals that threaten our lives, as our distant ancestors did, but we do feel attacked by their treatment of us.

Of course, we are not really in danger, but ego jumps in and says, "How dare you talk to me that way?" We allow the behavior of others to determine how we respond, as if kindness were a transaction, something that needs to be earned. When we do that, we give our power away.

**I believe that someone doesn't deserve my kindness.**

Our response is often determined by the judgments that we hold about others. It might be homeless people on the street or people who seem to be on drugs. It might be someone we see being rude to other people. It might be someone that we know has a different political view. We each have our own list.

We feel uncomfortable as we see these people on the street, and it's easier to avoid them or to ignore them as we pass. We allow our judgments to determine our response, and we make exceptions to the choice that we have made to live with kindness.

We make it about them, but it is always about us.

**We can choose to see through a kindness lens.**

Once we make a commitment to ourselves to live with kindness, over time, that becomes who we are. It takes practice.

If someone is rude to me or if I hold judgments about them, I can respond with kindness more easily if I shift the way I see them. I can look at them through a kindness lens. Then, I see them differently. I allow them to be as they are showing up now.

I do not know what's going on in someone else's life, but I can give them the benefit of the doubt and assume that they are dealing with challenges and doing the best they know how to do in this moment.

They do not need to earn my kindness.

When I choose to be kind, I am claiming my power to be who I want to be in the world. And that choice enriches my life.

We invite you to be patient with yourself as you try on your kindness lens, and we wish you joy on your kindness journey.

We're grateful that you are on this journey with us.

With love from our hearts to yours,

*Pat and Larry*

## Pebbles, Rocks and Sand – A Metaphor for Life

*Whatever choice you make makes you.*
*Choose wisely.*
                        ... Roy T. Bennett

Let's imagine a large glass jar. Next to it, a bowl of rocks - about 2 inches in diameter, a bowl of small pebbles, and a bowl of sand.

Let's imagine that we pour the sand into the jar. It fills a good portion of the jar.

Next, we pour the pebbles on top of the sand.

At this point, the jar is almost full, leaving little room for the rocks.

### Now, let's create a different scenario.

This time let's begin with the rocks, which easily fit in the jar.

Then, as we add the pebbles on top and shake the jar, the pebbles fill in the spaces between the rocks.

Finally, we add the sand, and as we shake the jar, the sand filters down between the pebbles, and everything fits nicely in the jar.

### The jar is a metaphor for life. – the time and space we have available to us.

The rocks are the most important things in our lives – our family and other relationships, our health, our personal wellbeing.

Pebbles are other things that matter too, such as our job, our education, the expression of the skills that we were born with, actions inspired by a sense of purpose.

Sand is the small stuff, ways we spend our time on activities that do not add significant value to our lives but take up time and space in our day, including hours of  TV watching. Most possessions fit here, also.

As I think about my life, I realize that I often get caught up in the pursuit of information that interests me. I seldom ask myself if this is a good use of my time. Looking back, I realize that I have allowed my various interests to take priority over activities that support my relationships with family and friends who matter most to me.

With that realization, I am reevaluating my priorities, no longer just following an interest without considering how I could use my time in a more fulfilling way. This is a shift to a new way of looking at my life, and it is a process that will unfold over time.

As I begin the process, I want to share a few thoughts

- This is not about right or wrong. It is about clarifying your priorities.
- Most of us get off track. Realizing it is the first step to shifting how you spend your time.
- Change of any kind is a process, so be patient with yourself.

You get to decide what the pebbles, rocks and sand represent for you.

You also get to decide if you want to make a change in how you spend your time.

Whatever decisions you make, we wish you a peaceful and fulfilling journey.

We're grateful that you are on this journey with us.

With love from our hearts to yours,

*Pat and Larry*

# We Are Each on Our Own Kindness Path

*Wherever there is a human being, there is an opportunity for kindness.*

Seneca

We are each living with the gifts and challenges of our life journey – perhaps similar, but different from those of any other person.

Once we have chosen to live with kindness, we are on a unique kindness path. What is right for one person may not be the right path for someone else.

There is no hierarchy of kindness, with some kind acts being more important than others. Every act of kindness adds a bit of love to our world, often changing someone's day at just the right time for them. Often, we do not know the impact of our kind word or action. A warm smile and pleasant greeting in someone's life at that moment might have a bigger impact than an elaborate plan to cheer someone up when they're down.

This not-knowing provides the foundation of our kindness practice. I am free to just show up with a genuine desire to connect, without analyzing someone else's situation and deciding if they even deserve my kindness.

For many people, kindness is a transaction. I will be kind to you if you are nice to me, or if I see you being kind to someone else. The other side of that coin is that I will withhold my kindness if you are rude to me or to someone else. I will judge you as unworthy of my kindness.

When that happens, I have moved from not-knowing to judgment, an easy step, but one that takes me out of my heart and leaves me off my chosen path. At that time, I give you the power to decide how I show up in this situation. Without knowing it, you are controlling my behavior.

Kindness is an expression of love. Withholding kindness happens when we have abandoned our heart and moved to our head, which is often full of judgments.

## How do we avoid that easy step?

Our actions are an expression of who we are. Once we decide to be kind – not just to act kind sometimes, but to be kind in the world - our actions follow that directive. Then, we do not respond in kind to someone else's behavior but with kindness, as an expression of who we are.

It takes practice. Most of us find it easy to fall back into judgment.

This is a good place to talk about our kindness journey. Always remember that it is a journey, a process. Like anything else in life, it offers us opportunities to grow as we go, to learn from the times when we fall short of our intended behavior. Sometimes, I still fall back into old patterns of reaction when I genuinely want to be kind. Some people still push my old judgment buttons.

Part of my journey has been learning to be kind to myself and to understand that the transition to being kind is a process. Letting go of the old way of being in the world takes time. The more we practice, the better we get at it.

So, be gentle with yourself. Welcome the times when you step off the path. Let them help you to understand yourself. Then return to the commitment you have made to yourself to be kind as you show up in our messy, challenging world again.

We're grateful that you are on this journey with us.

With love from our hearts to yours,

*Pat and Larry*

# An Upgrade to the Golden Rule

*Do unto others*
*as you would have others do unto you.*
The Golden Rule

How do you want to be treated? We each have an answer to that question, and our answers may have different details, but most can be summed up as being treated with kindness.

If you want to be treated kindly, the answer is simple: treat other people kindly. Of course, kindness has many expressions. A smile and pleasant comments are kind. Perhaps that is all that you would want from a stranger, so that is what you give. It forms a connection in the moment, and it is good for both of you.

The Golden Rule says, "Do unto others as you would have others do unto you," but that's not always enough. We need to upgrade to a Platinum Rule, where we "Do unto others as they would have us do unto them."

This is an overdue compassionate upgrade to the Rule.

The challenge with the original version is that it assumes that everyone else would need what I need, and more importantly, would not need what I do not need. The underlying assumption is that we are all alike; but in reality, we are vastly different in many ways, often not recognized even by good-hearted, kind people.

Kindness is love in action, and when we are guided by love, we relate to the other person with an openness to understand what they need. This goes beyond a passing pleasantry. It asks more from us.

If you move the rule from your head to your heart, then the upgrade makes sense in every circumstance. The question now becomes: "What is the most loving thing that I can do in this moment with this particular person in front of me?"

Kind acts are built on understanding what the other person needs. We often don't know, so we begin with something as simple as a smile and nod of the head.

I'm thinking now – and there are many other good examples – of people who are without homes, living on the street, usually because of situations in their lives beyond their control or conditions that are different from those that most people have to deal with.

In that case, what do they need that I do not? The first is empathy.

I am called to relate to them where they are, not projecting my life onto them, expecting them to respond to their challenges in the way that I would. If I had been walking their life journey, I would be different than who I am and I would respond differently to life's challenges than I do now.

For most of us, when we see someone who is struggling, we choose to ignore the person, because we don't know how to relate to them, or we don't want to get involved. But what if we knew that we could easily give them what they most want?

In recent surveys of people living on the street, researchers were surprised to find that what people wanted most was not food or medical care or a home, but just to be seen and acknowledged. Of course, their other needs were important, but being ignored as if they did not exist was the most painful part of their experience.

Knowing that helps us to step out of our comfort zone with a simple smile and greeting, not just for homeless folks, but for others as well. Making a human connection could change a person's day in ways we can't imagine.

Kindness can take many different forms, including acknowledging someone, listening to understand them, and relating to them as they are, without judgment.

If the initial greeting with a stranger went well, we might engage them in a conversation. As we learned more about their journey or their hopes and dreams, we would discover how much we have in common, and it might open the door for a next step - perhaps returning later with something they need.

That next step depends on how the first few minutes went. But even the smile and greeting has been a gift to them, and to you.

## An Invitation:

Are there people that you pass in your daily life without acknowledging them? Are you open to stepping out of your comfort zone?

We're grateful that you are on this journey with us.

With love from our hearts to yours,

*Pat and Larry*

## A New Way of Looking at Compassion

*If you want others to be happy, practice compassion.*
*If you want to be happy, practice compassion.*
~ Dalai Lama

Compassion, according to Merriam-Webster Dictionary, is a "sympathetic consciousness of others' distress together with a desire to alleviate it." In other words, we want to help when we are aware of the suffering of others.

Thinking about the role of compassion in our daily lives, I am reminded of an organization that came to my attention recently. With a clever grammatical twist, they call themselves "Compassion It," turning an adjective into an action verb.

As I explored their website and read articles about their activities, I was impressed by the impact they are having world-wide.

At the center of their practice is a wristband that says, "Compassion It." This is a gentle reminder not to react quickly in situations that usually elicit an impatient or unkind response from us. It creates the space for us to choose a compassionate response instead.

Our power is in that space. Typically, when someone triggers us, we think that the next step is our reaction to them., but there is a space between the stimulus and the response. Most of us do not realize that, so we don't take advantage of it. In that space, we can choose a compassionate response.

The wrist band reminds us to bring compassion to all interactions that we find ourselves in. We are prepared for kindness, rather than a habitual impatient or unkind response.

The wrist band serves another purpose as well. It prompts us to look for chances to bring compassion as we go through our day. It may be as simple as offering a smile and a few kind words to a stranger. You may feel moved to stop and have a brief conversation with a neighbor or a co-worker, thereby strengthening your connection. You might expand the reach of your kindness by volunteering with an organization that is having a positive impact on people's lives. The opportunities are limitless.

Compassion It is a 501(c)(3) nonprofit organization and global movement led by Sara Schairer and Burrell Poe. Their mission is "to inspire daily compassionate actions and attitudes," and their vision is "a world where compassion is practiced by every person, for every person, on every day."

Through their educational training and other tools, they are "empowering individuals and organizations to make compassion a priority."

**Workplace Compassion Programs**

Compassion It workshops focus on all employees, introducing key skills such as self-compassion, boundary-setting, and active listening. Compassion becomes part of the company culture.

Their Leadership Program helps the company to develop more compassionate and effective leaders. "Compassionate leaders show true concern for their employees, they value connection, and they listen with an intent to understand. This creates trust, loyalty, joy, and collaboration within a team."

**Personal Development Programs**

30-Day Compassion It Challenge

This easy to implement program offers 4 weekly lessons, each one focusing on a different aspect of compassion. The lessons are uplifting and easy to follow. Each one includes a video, interesting information and suggested actions to take during the week to embed the practice in your daily life.,

Many people have used this program in their schools, businesses, college campuses, and even in jails and prison yards.

Compassion Training for Busy People

This program takes an hour each week for connecting with others while you learn about and practice compassion and mindfulness. The hour includes brief lessons that cover the basics of the compassion training, breakout discussions and experiential exercises. It is followed by another half hour to continue the discussion.

## The Impact of Compassion It

Sara Schairer and Burrell Poe have led compassion workshops world-wide for people from all walks of life, including inmates in maximum security prisons and leaders in big tech companies.

They and their staff have distributed over 190,000 wrist bands in 50+ countries on 6 continents and in all 50 US states.

The global impact is impressive, and the impact on individuals and their families, schools and businesses is equally important. As more of us become committed to living with compassion, our communities become kinder and gradually, the culture changes. The more we commit to compassion in our lives, the more we will notice it showing up around us.

And our lives will be transformed in the process.

We're grateful that you are on this journey with us.

With love from our hearts to yours,

*Pat and Larry*

# A Kind Way to View People with Disabilities

*There is no greater disability in society than*
*the inability to see a person as more.*
Robert M. Hensel

At this point in my life, I cannot walk, and I use a wheelchair when I go out. Some people see me as being disabled. Although not able to do some of the things that I used to love doing, I am still very able to live my life fully. I am not disabled.

My experiences have given me a glimpse into the lives of other people who are experiencing a limited ability in some form. I have thought a lot about the way that people see those who are not functioning in the world in what is considered a normal way.

I looked for videos that could help me to shine a different light on the subject, and I was pleased to find a few that helped. I invite you to take a few minutes to watch them. I believe that you will be glad that you did.

There are a few basic guidelines that we need to know in order to relate to people with disabilities in a way that shows them respect.

*How to Talk to People with Disabilities*

Many people have embraced their disability and are living happy lives. They are not disabled. They are people first and they happen to have a disability, which is nothing to be ashamed of.

*Things People with Disabilities Wish You Knew*

In Indonesia, where most people thought that disabled meant useless, a young man with severe limitations did what seemed impossible. He became a successful photographer. He also designed and, with the help of his friends, built a car that he could drive.

*The Photographer with No Hands and Legs*

A young boy had a form of hyperactivity that he could not control, until a teacher, Mr. Jensen, saw in him what no one else could. It changed his life and set him on the path of a successful life and career.

Pat Downing

*Inspirational Video - Be a Mr. Jensen*
We're grateful that you are on this journey with us.
With love from our hearts to yours,
*Pat and Larry*

# The Power of Not-Knowing

*I think it's much more interesting to live not knowing
than to have answers which might be wrong.*
- Richard P. Feynman -

Have you ever noticed that sometimes what you know about someone gets in the way of your being kind?

Perhaps:

- they did something that you don't approve of, and you can't let go of it in your mind,
- you made an assumption about them based on the way they first showed up in your life,
- they belong to a political party that you don't like, so you just know that you could never trust them.

It's interesting to pay attention to the different ways that I decide who to be kind to and who to avoid. Often it has to do with assumptions that I have made.

Approaching anyone with not-knowing means putting aside the ideas that I hold in my mind and realizing that I don't know enough about them to judge them fairly. It means that if I knew why they were showing up the way they are right now, I would understand, and I would not judge them so harshly. I would choose to be kind.

This all goes back to remembering who I choose to be in the world. I choose to be kind, not just to do kind things. That is my aspiration, not the automatic reality in my day-to-day activities. I need ways to help my rational mind to accept this rather challenging assignment.

Remembering to see everyone through the not-knowing lens has helped me in several situations where I had strong judgments.

Now, I just assume that if I knew the person's life story, I would have compassion for them rather than the judgments that jump so easily into my mind. I see them through my not-knowing lens.

This decision arose, in part, out of several experiences with people who are often judged and excluded in our community because of assumptions that people make about them. As my husband, Larry, and I got to know some homeless folks, we heard the stories of their life journeys, and compassion replaced any judgments.

Sometimes, the way someone looks is a trigger for our assumptions. If someone is dressed in shabby clothing with dirty, worn shoes, we may see a person who is poor, too lazy to work, living on our tax money, maybe on drugs. It's enough to avoid them.

At the other end of the wealth spectrum, a man in a very expensive suit and shoes who drives a high-end car triggers judgments that he spends his money on frivolous things for himself, rather than paying his fair share of taxes or donating that money to organizations that help less advantaged people.

When people from nicer areas of town drive past a trailer park and see people outside, often they assume that they have less value than other people have. That attitude has long been expressed by the ugly term "trailer trash," as if financial means equals value as a human being.

So many triggers snap us into our judgment mode – a group of teenagers of another race hanging out on a street corner and "acting suspicious", a drug addict looking spaced out, a man with a mental disability walking by us, muttering out loud

There are so many situations that may trigger our judgments of people whom we see as others. But just how different are they from us? If we had been born into their family and had to walk their life journey, where would we be now. We wouldn't even be who we are today, because life experience helps to shape us.

Who would we be? How would we handle all the challenges that they have faced from childhood that helped to determine who they are today. We can't even say, "Oh, if that were me, I would ..." You wouldn't be who you are today, so you don't know what you would do.

This all brings us back to not-knowing as the way to move with grace and kindness in this world. It does not mean to put yourself in dangerous situations. I always check in with my intuition before entering an unfamiliar situation. But I invite you to experiment with the not-knowing mindset the next time you would normally avoid someone. Trust your intuition, and with practice, you'll be able to tell the difference between inner guidance and your over-active self-protective ego speaking.

I consider this a fun journey, learning more about myself and other people as I go. I invite you to give it a try. It will expand your world and, maybe, lead you to some new friends. It did for us.

That is our wish for you.

We're grateful that you are on this journey with us.

With love from our hearts to yours,

*Pat and Larry*

# That Could Be Me

*I think we all have empathy.*
*We may not have enough courage to display it.*
Maya Angelou

During the last few months, in our community and around the country, the homeless population has grown dramatically. As a result, more and more people are using online platforms and public meetings to complain that the presence of people living on the streets is having a negative impact on their lives. Many are fearful about the strangers who come into their neighborhood, seeing all of them as potentially dangerous. Of course, they want to feel safe for themselves and their families.

It becomes easy to see homeless people as dangerous and to blame them for the situation they are in. When we do that, we don't consider the economic and societal conditions that make it impossible for many people to stay in their homes and, in many cases, to get the medical and mental health support that they need.

There are many sides to this issue, and if we will ever resolve it as a society, we need to take all sides into consideration and come together to create solutions that meet everyone's needs. Government alone cannot create the needed services without the support of the community.

The solutions are not easy, but if we really want to live in a safe community, we all need to be part of the solution – at least in the way we view each other. Seeing another person as disposable is not a good starting point.

We need to begin by seeing that each person is doing the best he or she can:

- the person living on the street who is struggling to survive without basic necessities,

- the homeowner concerned about her safety and that of her children,
- the drug addict who is living in the prison of the addiction that controls his life,
- the politicians doing the best they know how to respond to this overwhelming crisis.

So how do we switch from our judgments to a more compassionate view?

When I see someone on the street who is clearly struggling, or I see someone behaving in a way that I don't approve of, I could judge him …

Or I could see him through a kindness lens.

**I could think, "That could be me."**

I could ask myself:

- If I had been born into the life that she was born into, who would I be now?
- What would my childhood have been like?
- What opportunities did I have that he did not have?
- What support systems that I have had, did she not have.
- What mental or physical disabilities does he have?
- What economic disruption in her life made it impossible to stay in her home?
- What natural talents was he born with that his life path did not enable him to develop, so he is not now enjoying the expression of those talents and being supported by them?
- Did he have anyone supporting and loving him as he grew up, or was he on his own, even as a child, to figure out how to survive in this world?

I don't know the answer to any of these questions, but the answers would help me to understand why he is showing up in the world now in the way that he is.

Those answers would open my heart and enable me to see him as another myself – another soul expressing in a human body– wanting to be seen and accepted, wanting to be loved and to express love, wanting all his basic needs to be met so he could have the space in his life to become the greatest expression of himself.

I think of the people in my life who supported and loved me and helped me to become the person I am. Who would I be today if his life path had been the one given to me?

So, when I say to myself, "That could be me," I open a space within me to love him rather than judging him. I find a way to reach out with compassion and show him kindness.

Who knows what impact a simple act of kindness will have on his life – or on mine?

Perhaps our encounter will be a blessing for both of us.

The next step is up to me.

In this powerful video, Rex Hohlbein shares the story of his joy and wonder when he stepped out of his comfort zone and discovered the beauty and humanity of homeless folks in his community.

I hope it will touch your heart as much as it did ours.

We're grateful that you are on this journey with us.

With love from our hearts to yours,

*Pat and Larry*

# You Are a Walking Neon Sign

*Identity is something that you are constantly earning.*
*It is a process that you must be active in.*
Joss Whedon

We are all energy beings. The energy of our mood and our current thoughts does accompany us as we move about in our day. It shows up in our posture, the expression on our face, the way we move and in the words we say and the tone of voice we use. We are a walking, visible expression of what we are feeling.

We are like a neon sign that says, "This is who I am."

It doesn't matter what words we use to define ourselves. Our actions speak for us.

What message do you want to broadcast?

Does your sign say, "I am kind," "I am compassionate," "I see you," or "I care about you"?

Does it sometimes say: "I am angry," "I am greedy," "I don't have time for you," or "I am right"?

We all get to choose the message that we broadcast. Our actions tell the world who we are in that moment.

A happy person comes in with a smile and an uplifting comment, and that is an invitation to engage. Angry or frustrated people send out different messages, often in a way that says, "Stay away from me today."

How do you usually show up? Are you friendly, with a smile and a pleasant comment? Do you ignore the people around you? Do you easily complain about the slightest inconvenience?

Your behavior has an impact on the people around you - sometimes uplifting, sometimes annoying or irritating.

Many of us usually show up friendly but can get triggered by the behavior of someone else and react with anger or a nasty comment. That is understandable. We have all done it. But is that who you want to be in the moment?

It isn't about them. It's about you.

Some say "I can't help it. That's how I am."

If that is what you think, I invite you to rethink that. You are in control of your actions.

Most of us present ourselves to the world and respond to other people in habitual ways. Our habits are so ingrained that it will require practice to change them. But, yes, you can change the way you react to others.

This takes us back to understanding the process of response. There is always a space between the other person's behavior and our reaction to it. In that space, we can pause and consider how to respond.

The incident triggers our interpretation of what it means, and then, we are reacting to the meaning that we have given it.

Decide not to react. Give yourself time to reframe the situation in your mind. Replace the meaning you have given the incident with a more positive thought that gives the other person space to show up in the way that he is in this moment.

Practice seeing the other person in a kinder light:

"He's having a bad day. I don't need to add to it."

"I don't know what's going on with her, but it's about her, not me"

"My response is about me, not him."

Then, your response might be as simple as ignoring whatever the other person said that triggered you. It might be a brief answer such as "I hear you" or some other neutral comment that does not lead to confrontation.

This is not excusing or condoning the person's behavior. It is about you maintaining your balance and continuing to be in the world in the way that you prefer to be.

So, how do we get there from where we are right now? It takes practice.

We need to be conscious of our current behavior and notice when we would like to go back and change how we just reacted. Notice it, but don't beat yourself up because you slipped back into your old habit. Changing habits takes time. Think of it as a useful, but enjoyable game that you have chosen to play with yourself.

It all goes back to who you want to be in the world and what you want your sign to say about you.

Who will you take out the door today? What will your sign say?

What would you like it to say?

We're grateful that you are on this journey with us.

With love from our hearts to yours,

*Pat and Larry*

## Can We Change Our Narrative?

*I always bow down to the so-called average person
who shows that, in fact, average human people can and do
change the narrative in a very profound way.*
- James O'Dea –

A narrative is a story that "connects and explains a carefully selected set of supposedly true events, experiences, or the like, intended to support a particular viewpoint or thesis"

What narratives are directing our thoughts and actions?

We all have personal narratives that help us to feel better about ourselves. They show up in job interviews, where we try to present the most positive picture of us, or in our memories of previous incidents in our lives that make us look like the good guy in whatever problems arose.

What narratives do I tell myself about other people? Have I bought into stereotypes that I have heard from other people? Are they true? Who am I excluding from my kindness because of those stories in my head?

We are surrounded by the narratives promoted by other people. Some are self-serving, but many have a larger purpose – to persuade us to their point of view. In most cases, we are unaware of the purpose behind the narrative, and also unaware of how much of it is true.

As more people accept a narrative, the more power it gains, and thereby entices others to believe it as real. We see this in many settings, perhaps most dramatically in politics.

Do you like the stories that are playing out in our lives today?

Let's take a closer look at how they work.

### The power of belief

We can learn a lot from knowing how placebos work.

In a study to determine the effectiveness of a new drug, participants do not know if they will get the drug or a placebo, a sugar pill. Researchers then record the results in terms of positive or negative responses in the patients.

In many cases, the placebo patients respond as well as those taking the drug. How can that be?

It is all about the belief or expectation that the patient holds.

Placebos are seen in other medical settings as well, especially if the patient has a serious disease. When the doctor is positive and supportive of living fully now, not predicting a negative outcome, the results are often more positive than the dreaded "odds." The belief in embracing life now contributes to a more positive outcome.

The other side of that coin is the power of the "nocebo." When doctors tell a patient that the odds are against them and that he or she has a certain amount of time to live, many people give up on life and prepare for death. By buying into the doctor's speculation about the unknown future, they create a belief against their own best interests. Studies have shown that patients have better outcomes when encouraged to live fully now than those who are given no hope.

**What narratives are we buying into in other areas of our lives?**

Many narratives are being promoted now in this country, and in the world, leading to increasing division, hostility, anger and hatred, when we so desperately need to remember how much we have in common.

This is the nocebo effect in our daily lives. As more and more people buy into the ideas of fear, hatred and division, they get caught up in the narratives. They do not realize it, because they have been led to believe whatever they are told by their trusted sources of "truth." They have given away their power to think for themselves.

If we all sat down with people of different political beliefs and just talked and listened to each other about our values and what we want for our lives and for our families, we would discover how much more we have in common than those things that separate us.

**It is time to change the narrative.**

We are more powerful than we realize to change the narrative and therefore, change the world.

Take the time to create a vision of what you want our world to be like.

Our vision is a world in which:

- we live together peacefully, with mutual consideration,
- our basic needs are met, including services for people with "special needs,"
- we all have access to a good education and meaningful jobs with fair wages,
- diversity is celebrated because of the richness that each person has to offer our communities,
- we remember our kinship and we act with kindness and generosity of spirit,
- the environment is protected from further destruction and policies have been implemented to restore what has been destroyed.

This is our vision. Yours may be different. Whatever it is, we invite you to write it down and decide how you can live according to that vision today, to help bring it into reality in the world.

It might require you to change your narrative about some people and then learn how to respond more positively when your paths cross. You might begin with a nod of the head and a kind greeting.

It might inspire you to become a volunteer locally or to speak out about an issue that you care about.

This transition happens slowly, and it begins with small steps. No matter how small a change you make, the more of us who join you, the faster we will see a difference in our communities and in the world.

Together we can make it happen. Let's create a narrative of a thriving world in which we live together with love and kindness and genuine concern for each other. Right now, wherever we are, we can begin to be the change that we wish to see in the world.

We will see an immediate positive change in our own lives, and we will participate in creating a larger change in the world.

We're grateful that you are on this journey with us.

With love from our hearts to yours,

*Pat and Larry*

# How Can We Include 'Difficult' People in Our Kindness Circles?

*The most rewarding things you do in life are often
the ones that look like they cannot be done.*
Arnold Palmer

Can we overcome beliefs that we hold that prevent us from being kind to some people?

It is so easy to exclude people we consider to be risky to engage or unworthy of our kindness, because of ideas that we have about them.

In response to last week's message, Maxine responded with a question for all of us to consider:

*"The following question I pose to all of us is how do we expand our circles to meet with and befriend those who are not in our usual community ... who are not easily in our small circles?*

*Then we can truly do as the song suggests -*

*I can't change the whole world,*

*But I can change the world I know,*

*What's within three feet or so."*

Let's explore this together. I invite you to share your ideas with us by leaving a comment below.

Larry and I have a few ideas that have worked for us in some circumstances, but we still haven't found a way to include everyone in our circle of kindness.

Our challenges are people who are always rude or are deliberately hurting others, and people whose actions cause harm to other people and to the planet.

We realized that looking at our personal interactions and national or global issues requires two different approaches. For today, let's focus on people whom we encounter in our daily lives – within three feet or so.

### What Narratives Do I Believe?

What stories do I tell myself about other people? Have I bought into stereotypes that are circulating in our community or in the nation? Are they true? Who am I excluding from my kindness because of those stories in my head?

My fallback example is our unhoused neighbors. Many communities are dealing with the challenge of increasing numbers of homeless folks living on the streets, with nowhere to go.

Negative narratives are being promoted now in this country, and in the world, about the homeless and other marginalized people. As more and more people buy into the ideas of judgment and fear, they get caught up in the narratives.

If we sat down with people who are living on the street and heard their stories, we would understand how they got to this point in their lives. We would be able to turn judgment into compassion, and from that, kindness would flow more easily.

**It is time to change the narrative.**

Part of your narrative is about who you are and how you fit into your picture of the world. Who do you choose to be?

Ask yourself, "Am I judging this person based on the one worst thing he ever did?" Does that really define who he is? If I knew his life story, I would understand why he is behaving in the way that he is, and I could more easily choose to have compassion for him.

You can change your narrative to reflect that choice.

It might inspire you to respond more positively when you cross paths with someone you had judged in the past. You could begin with a nod of the head and a kind greeting.

It might inspire you to become involved locally or to speak out about an issue that you care about. Now that you understand the larger issues that contribute to homelessness and the need for community involvement in addressing those needs, you might volunteer with a local agency that provides needed services.

This transition happens slowly, and it begins with small steps. No matter how small a change you make, the more of us who join you, the faster we will see a difference in our communities and in the world.

## The Power of Not-Knowing

Have you ever noticed that sometimes what you know about someone gets in the way of your being kind?

Perhaps:

- they did something that you don't approve of, and you can't let go of it in your mind,
- you made an assumption about them based on the way they first showed up in your life,
- they belong to a political party that you don't like, so you just know that you could never trust them.

It's interesting to pay attention to the different ways that I decide who to be kind to and who to avoid. Often it has to do with assumptions that I have made.

Approaching anyone with not-knowing means putting aside the ideas that I hold in my mind and realizing that I don't know enough about them to judge them fairly. It means that if I knew why they were showing up the way they are right now, I would understand, and I would not judge them so harshly. I would choose to be kind.

This all goes back to remembering who I choose to be in the world. I choose to be kind, not just to do kind things. That is my aspiration, not the automatic reality in my day-to-day activities. I need ways to help my rational mind to accept this rather challenging assignment.

Remembering to see everyone through the not-knowing lens has helped me in several situations where I had strong judgments.

Now, I just assume that if I knew the person's life story, I would have compassion for them rather than the judgments that jump so easily into my mind. I see them through my not-knowing lens.

This decision arose, in part, out of several experiences with people who are often judged and excluded in our community because of assumptions that people make about them. As my husband, Larry, and I got to know some homeless folks, we heard the stories of their life journeys, and compassion replaced any judgments.

Sometimes, the way someone looks is a trigger for our assumptions. If someone is dressed in shabby clothing with dirty, worn shoes, we may see a person who is poor, too lazy to work, living on our tax money, maybe on drugs. It's enough to avoid them.

When people from nicer areas of town drive past a trailer park and see people outside, often they assume that they have less value than other people have. That attitude has long been expressed by the ugly term "trailer trash," as if financial means equals value as a human being.

So many triggers snap us into our judgment mode – a group of teenagers of another race hanging out on a street corner and "acting suspicious", a drug addict looking spaced out, a man with a mental disability walking by us, muttering out loud

There are so many situations that may trigger our judgments of people whom we see as others. But just how different are they from us? If we had been born into their family and had to walk their life journey, where would we be now. We wouldn't even be who we are today, because life experience helps to shape us.

Who would we be? How would we handle all the challenges that they have faced from childhood that helped to determine who they are today. We can't even say, "Oh, if that were me, I would …" You wouldn't be who you are today, so you don't know what you would do.

This all brings us back to not-knowing as the way to move with grace and kindness in this world.

### Seeing Others Through a Kindness Lens

Most people are kind, but circumstances often determine when and where we express our kindness.

### Someone is rude to me.

It is natural for us to respond to other people in the way that they have treated us. Ego jumps in and says, "How dare you talk to me that way?" We allow the behavior of others to determine how we respond, as if kindness were a transaction, something that needs to be earned. When we do that, we give our power away.

### I believe that someone doesn't deserve my kindness.

Our response is often determined by the judgments that we hold about others. It might be homeless people on the street or people who seem to be on drugs. It might be someone we see being rude to other people. It might be someone that we know has a different political view. We each have our own list.

We make it about them, but it is always about us. It is about how we choose to show up in the world.

### We can choose to see others through a kindness lens.

Once we make a commitment to ourselves to live with kindness, over time, that becomes who we are. It takes practice.

If someone is rude to me or if I hold judgments about them, I can respond with kindness more easily if I shift the way I see them. I can look at them through a kindness lens. Then, I see them differently. I allow them to be as they are showing up now.

I do not know what's going on in someone else's life, but I can give them the benefit of the doubt and assume that they are dealing with challenges and doing the best they know how to do in this moment.

They do not need to earn my kindness.

When I choose to be kind, I claim my power to be who I want to be in the world. And that choice enriches my life.

We all have that choice. It uplifts our lives and the lives of the people we meet.

We're grateful that you are on this journey with us.

With love from our hearts to yours,

*Pat and Larry*

# The Everyday Spirit of Thankfulness

*Gratefulness allows us to nurture a keener eye*
*that no longer rushes past the small everyday moments*
*that make up the larger part of our lives.*
Guri Mehta

We often go through our lives without noticing the things around us that help to create the setting for our life experience. Most of the items in our home we have chosen because we thought that they would provide comfort or pleasure in some way. Then, they became the backdrop of our daily activities, and we no longer think about them.

I have read many articles suggesting that we make a list of things that we are grateful for. That is a helpful practice. Now I want to take it a step beyond noticing and listing.

## Going Deeper

Look around you. Focus on one thing that you are grateful for and think about it. Perhaps there is an interesting story about how it came into your life. Perhaps it belonged to a parent, and it brought with it pleasant memories. Perhaps you have used it in a way that created happy memories for you. Perhaps it makes your life easier or more enjoyable.

As you consider the role it plays in your life, it is not just an item on your list, but an experience of thankfulness. This goes beyond a process of the mind. It engages your heart and deepens your appreciation.

As we engage our inner spirit, we connect with the abundance that we have in our lives beyond the idea of how many things we have and how much they cost.

Family and friends often provide the primary abundance in our lives, bringing love, kindness, joy, support, wisdom, laughter, and so much more. This is the deeper abundance of the heart.

Coming together can be a sustaining, comforting part of our life, which is easy to take for granted.

In many cases, friends become more important than family in our daily lives. We may have more of a heart connection with a friend and share more personal beliefs and values with them than we do with family. When we are fortunate, we have close connections with both.

Stop and take a few moments to reflect on a friend or family member who has recently shown you kindness or for whom you have been kind. Kindness is one of the strongest ways of connecting with another person, whether we are giving or receiving kindness.

### Gratitude When Life is Challenging

Most of us have a vision of more in our lives than what we have right now. It's good to hold a vision of the next step for our life. It is also important to stay in gratitude for what we have now.

Sometimes life presents us with opportunities to grow and to expand beyond who we thought we were. In challenging times, we often focus on the disappointment we feel and overlook the many things for which we could be grateful, if we just noticed them.

Wayne Dyer said, "If you change the way you look at things, the things you look at change."

I have found that to be true.

I was the caregiver for both of my parents (separately). That required me to leave a career that Larry and I shared, that I enjoyed and that supported us financially. It was not even a decision. I just knew that it was the next step on my life journey, and I have never regretted it.

That opportunity enabled me to have a closer relationship with both of my parents. As challenging as it was at times, the opportunity to support them when they needed it deepened my connection to each of them.

That time reinforced for me a commitment to appreciate what I have in the moment and not to bemoan what I do not have.

I believe that we live in a circle of giving and receiving. Life shows us when it is a time for giving to someone who needs help, and we can find joy in the giving, without expecting anything in return. Of course, we do receive in so many ways, but that is not why we give.

The time may come when we also need help. In a circle, what goes around does come around to us again. I like this metaphor, because my whole life has demonstrated it – giving and then receiving from another source – and receiving, then later, having an opportunity to give to someone else.

At this moment in my life, I am in the receiving mode, and I have more joy and gratitude than at any other time that I can remember.

Several years ago, I was diagnosed with a progressive neurological condition that has gradually caused me to lose my balance and has altered the functioning of my body below the waist and in my head – resulting in changes in my eyesight, hearing, sense of smell and taste, speaking and also my ability to sing – which I miss. I am also not able to stand unsupported or to walk.

I had a choice – to curse my body or to continue to live in gratitude. It was an easy choice. I have to live with me, and who wants to live with a grump?

Instead of cursing my body, I love and appreciate it.

Instead of bemoaning my life, I live in gratitude:

- for my husband, Larry, who lovingly helps me to navigate in our home and when we go out,
- for our friends, who offer to help whenever I need extra help,

- for my son, David, and his wife and my three granddaughters who live near us,
- for the opportunity to live with joy and love and kindness, despite physical limitations,
- for the passionate work that Larry and I do to spread messages of kindness and to make a positive difference in the world.

This Tuesday, Larry goes to the hospital for a hip replacement. Several friends have rallied to provide transportation for him, to help me with my morning and evening transitions, and to bring me food and their company.

We truly have a lot to be thankful for on this Thanksgiving Day.

As we continue our journey, we learn new ways to live with more constant gratitude, which provides the foundation on which we build a life of joy.

We wish you love, gratitude and joy in this season of thankfulness, and in your entire life.

We're grateful that you are on this journey with us.

With love from our hearts to yours,

*Pat and Larry*

# What We Can Learn from Indigenous People

*"In our every deliberation, we must consider*
*the impact of our decisions on the next seven generations."*
Iroquois Maxim

No one living here today has any personal responsibility for the actions of the Europeans who settled in this land, but we owe it to ourselves to be aware of the history that led us to where we are now. This is not a history lesson, but history must be mentioned, because it is the backdrop of what we lost and what we can gain from the indigenous people who had lived in this land, in harmony with it, for centuries before Europeans came here.

It is an indisputable fact that the people who were here were living in harmony with the land that sustained them. Their lives were guided by values that can speak to us today, as we consider how we can stop the destruction of the earth and of one another in a struggle to survive in today's world that seems to be spiraling out of our control.

Suffice it to say that we have badly messed up the balance between ourselves and the living, intelligent planet that sustains us (to the extent that we allow her to do so). We have also failed dramatically in our relationships with one another.

We have so much to learn from those who lived here before us.

In the article, *Can the Indigenous Worldview Build a Better Future?* Vicki Zakrzewski asks:

- "Do we believe that every person, including those who are different from us, has intrinsic worth.
- Do we believe that the animals we love as pets and the ones who live in the wild have intrinsic worth?
- Do trees, rivers, oceans, mountains have intrinsic worth?
- If the answer is yes, then what should our actions be towards all these things and towards life itself?"

This presents us with an opportunity to consider our shared values and the choices that we are making as a people. It also invites us to consider our personal values and the choices that we make in our individual lives.

We can ask ourselves:

- Do I share the values of the indigenous people of the world?
- What values have I embraced to guide my life?
- Do my daily choices reflect those values?
- Which choices are not in harmony with those values?
- What changes can I make to enable me to live more in harmony with my values?

I know that this requires some reflection, so I invite you to come back to it when you have time, if you are so inclined. I also know that many people will not give it another thought, and that's okay. The choice is yours.

This is not a test. Very few of us live consistently by the values that we have chosen to guide our lives. We are human. We are all in a process of becoming more of who we can be.

This is an invitation to do some reflection, in whatever form that takes for you.

This is a time of thanksgiving. We all have so many things to be grateful for. For me, the opportunity to continue to grow is one. Times of reflection are a gift that I give myself.

I wish for you whatever helps you to live the life that you choose to live.

And I wish you joy every day.

We're grateful that you are on this journey with us.

With love from our hearts to yours,

*Pat and Larry*

## Meeting Today's Challenges with a Pandemic of Love

*When we give cheerfully
and accept gratefully, everyone is blessed.*
Maya Angelou

This week, as I was checking our "Nextdoor" feed online, I saw a post titled, *A Pandemic of Love Asheville.* Suzi Israel, who runs our local Pandemic with Love chapter, had posted the story of a young man whose life was changed because of local volunteers.

I shared information about the international Pandemic of Love organization in this blog in 2020, so this was a good opportunity to check in with them again to learn about their work in the world two years later.

Pandemic of Love is a grassroots, volunteer-led mutual aid community, started in March of 2020. "Mutual aid is a voluntary reciprocal exchange of resources and services based on the principle that members of a community should take responsibility for caring for one another."

In response to a growing need among her social media friends who were facing challenges due to COVID 19, Shelly Tygielski created a website to connect people in need with those who could help.

Pandemic of Love is powered by human connection. Since March 2020, their volunteers have connected over 1.2 million people to each other – "perfect strangers who reminded each other of our common humanity and that we need each other in order to survive and thrive."

Each week, they get hundreds of new stories of connection – "stories of hope and triumph, stories that uplift and inspire."

While Pandemic of Love was initially formed to provide financial help to people in need due to pandemic-related income loss, the organization has been expanding through local micro-community chapters to meet the different needs that are arising at this time.

*"Our team of volunteers are partnering with brands and organizations, assisting communities-in-need, and joining forces with global movements with the intention of creating sustainable, formalized mutual aid communities all across the world, long after the pandemic is over."*

It is easy to become involved if you are inspired to do so. Once you find a chapter in your area, you can click on links to offer or to receive help. Then, spread the word locally.

**So, let's return to Asheville.**

Earlier this week, Suzi Israel wrote:

*"In the summer of 2020, Chance registered for assistance. I called him immediately. He was 19 and homeless. His story broke my heart, a young man abandoned by those who should have loved him, and he had nowhere to go. I immediately called Shelly Tygielski, our founder, and we went to work to get him the help he needed.*

*Something about Chance just grabbed our hearts. We became his 'Pandemic Moms.' Chance has grown with love and encouragement and finding a family of his own in the last 2 years. I check in with him and he checks in with me when he needs to. Last weekend he finally got to meet his 2nd Pandemic mom face to face. It was wonderful to see him and get a big hug.*

*I am passionate about the work (that is not work to me) I do with Pandemic of Love because of people like Chance"*

**This is how we navigate these challenging times.**

This is a time when we all have opportunities to reach out and help one another. Pandemic of Love is one of many. We have found joy in being of service to people in need of help, and also in receiving help when we need it. We think of this as the Circle of Kindness.

Our hope for you is that you find an outlet for your kindness, and that you experience the gifts that come from being in that circle.

We're grateful that you are on this journey with us.

With love from our hearts to yours,

*Pat and Larry*

## You are Creating the Future,
## Not Just for Your Life, but for the World

*We can't heal the world today, but we can begin
with a voice of compassion, a heart of love, an act of kindness.*
~ Mary Davis

Do you believe that you have an influence on the future of the world? I believe that we do, and when we realize this, we take our daily choices more seriously.

At a time when you find yourself feeling offended or in judgment of someone in front of you, ask yourself:

"Would I want to live in a world in which everyone was acting in the way that I am about to act?"

That may be the most important decision that you can take – to stop and consider your response to any situation before you.

We all act by habit. When we respond to certain situations the same way day after day and year after year, that pattern becomes so programmed in our brains that we never think about what we will do next. It's already in our body, ready to express in the next moment.

Are you happy with your automatic reactions, or would you prefer to be more thoughtful of others or more patient or kinder to other people?

It's helpful to consider these questions after an interaction in which you reacted from habit:

"How do I feel about how it turned out?"

"Was I kind, or did I show up as someone whom I would not want in my life?"

How do you want other people to show up in your life?

Think about it. Write it down. Consider it during the day and go back and add to the list as you get more clarity.

Now ask yourself, "Is this the way that I am showing up in my daily life?"

If not, ask yourself, "What can I do to improve my interactions with others?"

Pat Downing

## The Jigsaw Puzzle of Humanity

In the worldwide jigsaw puzzle of humanity, each person is one piece of the puzzle. We each add to our puzzle piece every day. What do I want mine to look like?

What do I want to add to the larger picture?

Do I want my piece to add to the beauty of the picture or is it okay with me if my contribution adds to the chaos and ugliness of the picture?

It all comes down to deciding who I want to be in the world and then consistently expressing myself in that way, as much as I can, every day.

If you decide to be more kind, then make that your focus.

The more you choose to live with kindness, the more it becomes a habit, a part of you.

Then one day, you will discover that you have become kindness. It is not just what you do. It is who you are.

Now you have become love in action.

Be patient with yourself when you fall short of your intended kind response to someone else. Even when we plan to live with kindness, most of us meet people with whom we find it very difficult to be kind. That is part of the process.

Life is a journey, not an event.

Every day brings us opportunities to expand, to become more of who we want to be.

For every encounter in which I respond in a way that is kind, I feel good. Every time I have not been considerate of someone else, I take the time later to replay it in my mind so I can see why I reacted with judgment or impatience or lack of consideration of the other person.

Then I imagine myself having a kinder response. No longer in the heat of the moment, I can imagine another response and a better outcome. That becomes my template for the next challenging encounter.

I know the challenges will keep coming, because an important way that we can grow is through practicing the hard stuff.

I believe that there is a loving power in our lives that provides us opportunities to become more of who we are capable of being. The more that we set an intention for our lives, the more opportunities appear to move us forward on that path.

As a result, we find that our lives flow more easily, and more people respond positively to us.

In addition, the world becomes kinder. Think about that puzzle piece. It is surrounded by other pieces – people who are around us as we go through our day.

As our lives become kinder, our puzzle pieces become brighter and more beautiful. People interacting with us are impacted by the kindness that we offer, and their contributions become brighter as well. Then, the people around them are influenced by their increasing kindness, and our place in the puzzle becomes kinder, more inclusive, more compassionate and brighter.

As our little corner of the world is becoming brighter, millions of people around the world are making similar choices and creating other bright spots in the puzzle. All of those bright spots keep growing, as more and more people respond to the invitation to be a part of the emerging kinder, brighter world.

Imagine the picture that we can create together.

Now, when you consider the future, what do you see?

Don't tell me about what you see on the news. Right here is real life. This is where the changes are happening – one life at a time - all over the world. This is the unreported transformation of humanity.

You don't believe it? Just wait and see.

While you're waiting, we invite you to get clear about what you want the world to be like, then get out there and live it, and enjoy the changes in your life.

We're grateful that you are on this journey with us.

With love from our hearts to yours,

*Pat and Larry*

# Reflections on Giving and Receiving

*When we give cheerfully and accept gratefully,*
*everyone is blessed.*
Maya Angelou

This is a season of giving and receiving. In our hurried lives, we often get so caught up with the making or buying, then wrapping and maybe mailing of gifts, that it becomes more of a chore than a celebration.

For many people, the season brings unfulfilled expectations, or feelings of guilt at not having the time or the means to provide the kind of gifts that they want to give to others. We need to reevaluate what giving and receiving can be and how to make it more of a celebration, no matter what form it takes.

## The Joy of Giving

When I was a child, my family had a tradition of making Christmas gifts for friends and relatives. I have good memories of the kitchen table full of candles to be decorated, sequins, ribbons, and tiny straight pins to attach the decorations to the candle. That was a one year's project. Each year, Mother gathered the makings for a different creative offering, and my brothers and I dug in and created our unique works of art.

As we grew older, and our parents were able to afford the extra expense, we moved on from our creative endeavors to buying our gifts. That was fun, also, as we learned to look thoughtfully for just the right present for everyone on our list. It required us to think about each person as we shopped and to consider what each one would enjoy receiving.

One of my favorite memories is baking Christmas cookies with Mother. I still have her Betty Crocker Cookie cookbook, well-worn and dilapidated, decorated by remnants of cookie dough and full of happy memories.

As an adult, I continued the tradition of giving home-baked cookies. I imagine that every cookie carries some of the love that I put into the making of them.

As my life unfolded, with all its ups and downs. I always came back to the pleasure of giving something that I created. Whether in exchange for or in addition to store-bought gifts, I always felt that it was the best way to express my love.

## The Joy of Receiving

To truly experience the receiving of a gift, savor the moment.

Consider how the gift was selected or created by the giver, then wrapped and prepared for you to have the pleasure of unwrapping their offering. This is a moment of connection – not just with the gift, but also with the giver, whether they are present or far away.

Now relate to the gift. Consider how it will enhance your life - perhaps make it easier or more enjoyable. Perhaps it will give you pleasure, perhaps meet a need.

Then, of course, we also receive presents that do not do any of those things. How do we receive an unwanted gift? We can choose not to make it about the gift, but about the giver and about who we choose to be, in the moment, as a gracious receiver.

I can feel disappointed and wish for something that I wanted, or I can feel gratitude for the intention of the giver to give me something that pleases me. The gift is not the important thing. Our connection is.

It always comes back to who I want to be, not about a particular gift.

Perhaps the gift came from a former friend or a relative with whom I no longer have a relationship. It would be easy to disregard it and not acknowledge their thinking of me. But it might be a way to heal an old misunderstanding. Gifts are door-openers, and we always have the choice of whether or not to walk through that door and to heal what was broken. Again, I always get to choose how to respond.

In our culture, there is a healthy tradition of passing on to someone else gifts that we do not use. It provides us a thoughtful outlet for the disappointment of not receiving what we would have preferred. I am sure that I was the recipient of such a gift more than once, and I suspect that one fruitcake made the rounds among our family and friends for years.

A word of caution: keep a record of who gave you an unwanted gift. You want to be sure to find someone else to pass it on to.

**What Does It All Mean?**

There is an idea in our culture that gifts between people are supposed to be of equal value. I consider gift-giving in the same way that I consider kindness. Neither is a transaction in which the giving and receiving must be measured and carefully balanced. We are kind because that is who we are, not because of what we want in return. We give gifts freely, because it is a way to express our affection or appreciation for one another, not to ensure that we get back something of equal value.

Some of my favorite gifts have been handmade: a beautiful wall hanging from my brother, Bob, and delightful works of art from our granddaughters, Sydney and Mia. Their value cannot be measured financially. They represent something deeper, a heart connection that enriches my life.

So, where do we go from here?

I invite you to consider your own giving and receiving:

- Can you give yourself a break and not try to meet other people's unrealistic expectations of you?

- Can you see the value in what you are able to offer to others and in what you receive from them
- – all as expressions of something more important than the gifts themselves?
- Can you see all of this as part of the dance of life and a celebration of our being here together on this wonderful planet?

We wish you joy in the process of giving and receiving and love in every day of your life.

We're grateful that you are on this journey with us.

With love from our hearts to yours,

*Pat and Larry*

# Commitment to Kindness Becomes a Way of Life

*Continue to be who and how you are,*
*to astonish a mean world with your acts of kindness.*
Maya Angelou

When we make the choice to live with kindness, we are choosing a way of life that invites us to think differently about how we meet each day. That choice brings with it a commitment to start where we are and to be more aware of opportunities to be kind as we go through our day.

## Planting Seeds

Every act of kindness is like a seed that we are planting in our world, knowing that each one helps to create the kinder world that we envision. Often, we receive immediate feedback in the form of a smile or a pleasant comment in return, but sometimes, we do not get a response. It is helpful to remember that we are planting seeds, and seeds need time to grow.

We are all planting seeds of some kind, and we get to decide what kind of seeds we're planting. When we choose seeds of kindness, in time, we will reap an abundant harvest in our lives, but we won't see many others who will benefit in their lives from the seeds that we planted.

## Commitments to Ourselves

As we keep planting those seeds, it is helpful to develop habits that support expanding the reach of our kindness practice. We can make commitments to ourselves:

### To be aware of opportunities to be kind

A key to a satisfying kindness journey is staying conscious of the people around us. When we stay present in the moment, we notice people and we can see ways to respond to them with kindness.

It may be as simple as smiling and acknowledging someone or making a pleasant comment. It might be inviting someone behind us in line to go ahead of us or stepping up to help someone by opening a door or carrying something for them. It may, at times, require more of us.

We get to decide in every encounter how to respond.

**To acknowledge kindness when we receive it or observe it**

There are no insignificant acts of kindness. Every small act of kindness matters. For many people, small kind acts are their way of being in the world.

When we receive their kindness, it is so easy to thank them. Beyond that courtesy, we like to say, "You are very kind," as an acknowledgment. Sometimes, we tell them our favorite definition of kindness – "Love with its work boots on," and then say, "That is you."

We each have our own way of receiving kindness. It is part of the joy of the kindness path.

**To graciously receive other people's kindness**

Many of us are so used to being self-sufficient that we automatically turn other people's kindness away. It is easy to reject an offer of help, saying, "I'm fine, thanks," even if a little help would be welcome.

One evening, we were with friends at a local Waffle House restaurant. While we were enjoying our meal and each other's company, two men from the table behind me were leaving, and one of them presented me with a large feather, without a word. Taken by surprise, I thanked him, then he was gone before I could say anything else. To this day, that feather reminds me of the kindness of a stranger, and it has a special place on my desk.

Kindness is a circle, always in flow. If no one is willing to receive kindness, no one will be able to give it. I hope the stranger with the feather felt the joy that I experienced in receiving his gift.

As an aside: Larry says, "Remember to make an occasional trip to a Waffle House and mingle with the salt of Earth."

**To look honestly at ourselves**

Setting time aside for reflection is helpful as we navigate our kindness path.

Looking back at the end of the day helps me to see:

- When was I kind and to whom?
- How did it feel?
- Where was I hesitant to be kind and why?
- Who am I excluding from my kindness?
- What judgments in me prevent me from being kind?

I can ask myself:

- "What could I do next time to overcome the hesitance that prevented me from being kind this time."
- "What am I afraid of?"
- "Why?"

This process of reflection helps us to understand ourselves better, so we can be more comfortable the next time life presents us with similar encounters. It helps us to decide when and how to expand the circle of our kindness.

**To be kind to ourselves in the process**

There is no right or wrong way to walk a kindness path. We each get to choose our way of bringing love out into the world. It is important that you're kind to yourself, not asking more than you are comfortable giving at this moment.

We invite you to commit to whatever level of kindness that you choose. Then, when you are ready, you may want to take it up a notch – going from kindness in comfortable situations to those that are more challenging. It can be a bit scary, but also exhilarating when we step out of our comfort zone.

We thank you for choosing to bring your kindness out into a world that needs all the love it can get. You do make a difference with every act of kindness.

We're grateful that you are on this journey with us.

With love from our hearts to yours,

*Pat and Larry*

# Do We Belong to Each Other?

*Tomorrow belongs to those of us*
*who conceive of it as belonging to everyone,*
*who lend the best of ourselves to it, and with joy.*
Audre Lorde

I have been pondering this question lately – Do we belong to each other?

When we think of belonging, we usually think of owning something – that car belongs to me or this coat is mine. That means that I am in control of it. But there's also another meaning of belonging. It's not a possession kind of belonging. It is a deep connection, a soul connection, something that uplifts us and sustains us through difficult times

My first conscious realization of this kind of belonging came to me through my relationship with Sue Sikking. Sue was a close family friend. When I was just two years out of college, I moved to California to begin a job in Palos Verdes. Sue was minister of the Unity Church in Santa Monica, and I was often able to spend weekends with her. During every visit, she shared her heart and her wisdom with me. From that relationship, I learned many things about myself and about how best to navigate my often-challenging life journey.

Years later, when my children were teenagers, we were on vacation in California. I visited Sue, who was then in a nursing home because of her advanced Alzheimer's. I was warned that she would probably not remember me. When I approached her as she sat alone in her wheelchair, she looked up at me, gave me a radiant smile and said, "You belong to me!" "Yes, I do," I said, fighting back tears that were a mixture of grief and joy. We had a heart connection that was greater than the power of her physical condition.

Later that day, I was able to join her for lunch. By then, she did not remember who I was. She could not feed herself, and I was able to spoon feed her. After a while, she looked at me and said,

"Take me home with you." I told her that if I could, I would, as I fought back tears.

That was one of the most uplifting and heart-breaking days of my life. To this day, whenever I look at her picture on my desk, I say, "Yes, Sue. I belong to you."

Recently, Larry and I have been exploring the idea of belonging to one another. We feel a sense of belonging when we're with close friends or family members with whom we have a heart connection. Our larger intention is to expand our sense of belonging to include everyone we meet. Can we see each one as a part of our larger family, with whom we are connected at a deeper level, no matter how they are showing up in this moment?

This requires us to let go of our judgments about their behavior in this moment and to see the larger picture of our shared humanity. We really are in this world together. Imagine how different the world would be if we remembered our kinship, instead of focusing on the differences that keep us apart and help us to see each other as enemies.

We all have the power to help create the emerging world as one of connection and belonging. The choices that we make every day will determine how quickly that world will emerge from the chaos and disconnection that we see around us.

Now is the time to claim our power and to live in the realization of our oneness, to the best of our ability. You may not see the whole world changing, but you will see your part of the world taking on a new lightness, as you reach out with love in each encounter and feel that love flow back to you.

We're grateful that you are on this journey with us.

With love from our hearts to yours,

*Pat and Larry*

# Finding Your Power at a Time of Uncertainty.

*The secret of change is to focus all of your energy,*
*not on fighting the old, but on building the new.*
Socrates

As we continue to see extreme divisions in the United States, most of us are still trying to make sense of the outpouring of hatred and violence that is threatening a peaceful way forward.

This is the culmination of politics that for years was designed to divide us through messages of hate and fear, and recent rhetoric that was designed to turn that hate and fear into violent action.

As a result, the stability of our government and our society is at stake.

As I was sorting out my thoughts and feelings about what I see happening to our country, I came across a message from Krista Tippett of The On Being Project

Krista wrote:

*"We are creatures made, again and again, by what would break us."*

I believe that she is right.

This is a time that could break us. It will also give us the opportunity to find the strength and wisdom within us to meet the challenges. When enough of us do that, we will be transformed, and so will our world.

But, at the moment, it feels like a time of darkness in our country and around our planet.

I am reminded of a message from Valarie Kaur, founder of The Revolutionary Love Project. She asks us to consider: Is what we are experiencing "the darkness of the tomb or the darkness of the womb."

I like the analogy of the womb. As the time of birth approaches, the mother reaches a point of severe pain, with contractions coming rapidly, one after another. Many women have said it felt like dying.

The technical term for that part of the birth process is transition. The mother is reminded to breathe through the pain. Soon after, she gets the urge to push the baby out. As hard as it is, she is told to push through the pain.

Breathe, then push. Breathe, then push.

Soon, a new life is born.

If we can see the transition we are going through now as the birth of a new world, we can see that the turmoil and chaos will pass. The good news is that we each get to contribute to what comes next.

Breathe. Take long, deep breaths to get your balance.

Then push. Take whatever action you can take to support the birth of the new world that you want to see rise out of the chaos.

We are being called to counter hate and fear with the transforming power of love, which shows up in every act of kindness, no matter how big or small it may seem. We are already having a positive impact on the world.

This is not a time to assume that we cannot make a difference. Every act, every thought we think, and every word we speak, enters the morphic field in which we live. That energy field affects the direction of our planet.

This is a time to claim the power of love, knowing that we can help to birth the new world that will emerge from the chaos.

We wish you joy as you contribute to the birthing of a kinder new world.

We're grateful that you are on this journey with us.

With love from our hearts to yours,

*Pat and Larry*

# Love is a Powerful Force in the World

*Your task is not to seek love, but merely to seek and find*
*all the barriers within yourself that you have built against it.*
Helen Schucman

The subject of love intrigues me. Many articles or videos come to my attention every week, and I am easily pulled in.

Last week, an interesting article left me pondering the question: "What is the opposite of love?"

## Does Love Have an Opposite?

We, in our world of duality, seem to need to place things neatly in relation to one another, either like or unlike, the same or opposite. Of course, in our complex world, most things, ideas or feelings do not have an opposite. But let's think about the opposite of Love.

Many people consider Hate to be Love's opposite. Others say that it is Fear. In her article, *Mighty in Contradiction*, Patty de Llosa wrote:

*"In my understanding the opposite of love is power. Love accepts and embraces. Power refuses and crushes opposition. Love is kind and knows how to forgive. Power is competitive and takes others into account only when it stands in the Winner's Circle."*

This is a good accounting of Love's qualities, but it seems terribly unfair to Power. I believe that Power is neutral. It can be used for good or evil. I believe that Love is a Power and can be a strong counterforce to Power that is used for any purpose that takes from others for selfish reasons.

## What Would Love's Opposite Be?

So, that brings me back to the interesting question: If Love has an opposite, in our three-dimensional world, what would it be? I asked our friend Michael, and his answer was the one that makes the most sense to me.

Indifference.

How often do we or others completely ignore people we pass, without even acknowledging that they exist? How often do we hear about people who are suffering from injustice or facing life threatening challenges, and we don't give them a thought. We don't hate them or fear them. Those responses require us to see them, to be aware of them as fellow humans.

When we are indifferent, we wipe them out of our awareness. Is that Love's opposite? It's the closest I have heard. But this is all just a semantic exercise.

**I do not believe that Love has an opposite.**

I believe that Love is the unifying principle of all life. It is that from which all things and all of us emerged, and I believe that it is an innate impulse in all living things.

Of course, in this three-dimensional world, our ego minds have the ability to override our natural inclination to come together and to live in harmony with one another. That's part of the wonderful, scary, uplifting, challenging, rewarding dance that we all get to experience in this world.

I believe that we are never separated from Love. It is our true essence and our deepest impulse. This idea is expressed beautifully by Daniel Nahmod in his song, *One Power*. Daniel's message is that whatever names we give to the God or other power that we recognize in our lives, they are all expressions of the One Power.

**How Do We Access This Power?**

Most of us have an inner yearning to live lives of love and belonging and joy. As we learn to express the love that is within us, acknowledged or unseen, we develop our personal power to live the lives that we long for.

No matter how many challenges we face in today's world, I believe that Love is the most effective antidote to counter the forces of hate, fear, greed and indifference that seem to have taken over the world.

Love doesn't get much press, but throughout the world, more and more, people are choosing Love as a way of life. It is a grassroots global movement, and it is vibrant and growing under the radar.

You are already a part of this powerful force for good.

Thank you for being a shining light that brightens the way for others.

We're grateful that you are on this journey with us.

With love from our hearts to yours,

*Pat and Larry*

# When Feeling Sad or Overwhelmed

*When I despair, I remember that all through history,*
*the way of truth and love have always won.*
- Mahatma Gandhi

During the last week, I felt myself being pulled into a feeling of frustration, even a bit of overwhelm, as I faced several challenges that I could not figure out how to resolve.

As I looked for music to help me shift my mood, a song from Carrie Newcomer spoke to me and brought me to a place of balance and gratitude.

In *Three Feet or So*, Carrie reminded me of what I knew, but had lost sight of as I sank into my frustration.

I had gotten so focused on problem solving that I forgot my usual mood shifter. Gratitude has helped to bring me back to balance many times, and this time, it did, too. But first, I had to release the frustration that I felt.

Larry is a great sounding board. He listened as I shared with him the thoughts that I was having and feelings that they triggered in me. That enabled me to release emotions that were interfering with my ability to see the obvious solutions to the problems that I was trying to resolve.

When I have built up emotions, it helps me to vent. Larry is a good listener, and I can always count on him to sit with me and just listen as I express whatever is in me that needs to come out.

That was all I needed to get my balance back. Then, I thought about the many things for which I am grateful. As I spoke them out loud, I returned to a sense of wellbeing.

With that new mindset, I was able to see the obvious solutions that my frustrated mind had not been able to see. It was a good reminder to me to catch myself as I begin to feel frustrated and to take a break - do something relaxing or uplifting to shift my energy back to wellbeing.

If you don't have anyone with whom you feel safe expressing what you're feeling, you might want to talk out loud to yourself, or write it on paper or in the computer, then burn it or erase it with the intention of releasing it from your life.

When life seems overwhelming, we may have to dig deep to find anything that we are grateful for. Even when current challenges are dominating our thoughts and feelings, when we think about the big picture of our life, we realize that we have many things for which we are thankful, beginning with the breath in our body that keeps us alive.

When we act with kindness, we tap into the love within us. We believe that Love is our essential nature, and kindness is the way that we express it in the world every time that we give it an opening.

Love is the reason that we have a yearning for connection with others. It is the impulse that causes us to smile at another person, to learn their name and to listen to their stories.

Every act of kindness is an expression of love.

None of us can change the world. That is not our job. We believe that we are called on to decide what we will add to the world, then, to focus on doing that in a way that feels right to us.

By changing what we bring to what is in front of us, we have an impact on others. Acts of kindness create ripples that go out from them and affect the people to whom we are kind and, also, those who witness our kindness. How any of them respond is up to them. We will never know the full impact, if any, of our actions. We don't need to know.

You may feel called to join an organization or a group that is working to bring supplies, support or services to people in need. If so, you are widening your circle of kindness beyond three feet or so. That is an important way to be of service, but nothing is more important than how we interact with those who are right in front of us.

Who would you like to include in your circle of kindness?

What sparks an impulse in you to reach out to someone with kindness?

It's up to each of us to decide how to respond to the impulse within us to reach out to others with love.

We wish you joy on your journey, as you continue to take your love out into the world.

We're grateful that you are on this journey with us.

With love from our hearts to yours,

*Pat and Larry*

# The Power of Love in Response to Addiction

*What seems to us as bitter trials
are often blessings in disguise.*
Oscar Wilde - Irish Poet

This morning, I listened to an inspiring presentation by Killian Noe, the founding director of The Recovery Café Network. She offered ideas on "Living with Hope in the Darkness of Our Time," and her comments relate to our work with kindness as well as her work with clients who have addictions.

Recovery Cafes offer a safe place where people with addictions can go to be part of a community that accepts them as they are and offers them support on their healing journey.

Killian told a true story about Mahatma Gandhi that really spoke to me. A boy in India was addicted to sugar, and he was stealing candy and other sweets wherever he could. A friend suggested to his mother that she take him to see Gandhi. The mother and her son walked almost a whole day to reach Gandhi's ashram.

When the mother explained to Gandhi that her son was addicted to sugar and needed his help, Gandhi asked her to come back in two weeks. She did not understand why he could not help them while they were there, but they did return two weeks later.

When Gandhi saw the boy, he said to him, "Stop eating sugar."

The mother was surprised and a bit annoyed. She asked why he did not just say that during their first visit.

Gandhi replied, "Because two weeks ago, I had not given up sugar myself. and I could not ask anyone to do what I was not committed to myself."

Wow! That got us thinking about the increase of addiction in our culture and the criticism and judgments around people who are addicted, especially to opioids and other drugs.

We thought about what we expect from other people that we are not committed to ourselves.

We thought about the many ways that we and others are addicted, either to substances or attitudes and behaviors that are habitual in our daily lives.

That opened a Pandora's Box that many of us would not want to look in.

We began by asking ourselves:

What am I addicted to?

What people do I judge for their addictions?

Those questions do not apply only to physical addictions to sugar, alcohol and drugs, but also to attitudes and judgments of others whose personal choices and lifestyle are different from ours.

In our culture, most of us have some attitudinal, as well as physical addictions. We realized years ago that an attitude or tendency to judge others, over time, becomes an addition. We keep feeding it every time we see a person doing whatever it is that we do not approve of. It arises in us as an automatic response.

So, this brings us back to where we are now.

Am I willing to sit with these questions and truly look at myself?

Am I able to replace my judgments with love and kindness?

What would that look like?

At the Recovery Café, when someone with an addiction walks in the door, they are welcomed with the greeting, "You are loved. You are not abandoned."

For the people entering that door, their addiction has brought them a blessing they had not expected – a community of people who will love them and support them, no matter what their challenges might be.

Are we able to say words of welcome to those whom we now judge or condemn for who they are or how they show up in life?

Does it matter to us to be able to do that? We each get to answer that for ourselves, in our own way.

At the very least, let's admit to ourselves that we also have our limitations. How would we want people to respond to us, even if they knew what we know about our own shortcomings?

Can we bring love and kindness where before we brought disdain and judgment?

Sometimes, when we have chosen to live with kindness, life asks a lot from us. We all get to choose how we respond.

Our job is to offer opportunities to consider. You get to take any next step when you are ready. A kindness path does not demand anything from us. It offers us opportunities, and we each meet them in our own way.

We wish you joy and peace as you walk your kindness path.

We're grateful that you are on this journey with us.

With love from our hearts to yours,

*Pat and Larry*

# What Is Your Intention for Your Kindness Journey

*"I've found that 20 percent of any change is knowing how, but 80 percent is knowing why."*
Tony Robbins

Larry and I talked a lot this week about our intention for our life together and for our Kindness work. We realized that our big "Why" is to help create the world we envision - a world in which people are kind to one another and live with love and acceptance.

## What is Your Intention for Your Life?

We envision a world in which people live together peacefully, with love and kindness. Our intention is to live our daily lives being mindful of opportunities to bring that vision to life with our thoughts and words and actions.

We remember a time when we had a bluebird nest box on a pole in our backyard. With a high-powered camera lens, we could see the activity up close. We were delighted at watching the progress as the pair brought twigs and other materials to build a nest in the box, and then, as the male brought food to the female as she sat on the eggs in the nest. Soon, came the flurry of activity once the babies were hatched, as both parents flew out to find food for their young ones.

We really appreciated our up-close view when the young ones were feeling the urge to fly. They took turns standing just inside the opening of the box and spreading their wings as if they were about to fly. Then, they would back up as if saying, "I don't feel ready yet."

Of course, the birds had no such thoughts. They were simply following the natural calling in them to take the next step for their lives. Soon, they had fledged, and we had the joy of witnessing that victory of nature.

That memory brought us to the question: What is our natural calling?

We feel called to bring love and joy into the world as an antidote to the hate and fear that is so prevalent around us today. Our intention to live with kindness arose from that deep calling.

## Our Attention Supports Our Intention

How do we live in harmony with our intentions?

We start by paying attention to our responses to everything and everyone who crosses our path today. Then, we can see what we can do to expand our capacity for kindness.

We all have blocks within us that limit our ability to be kind in some situations. We are human, and we have habitual behaviors that come naturally in certain circumstances. Paying attention as we go through our day will help us to notice opportunities to break out of those patterns.

If we notice that we usually ignore certain people, for instance, we may decide to acknowledge them the next time we see them. That may require letting go of our resistance to them, based on some preconceived ideas about who they are.

Taking a few minutes every evening would provide you an opportunity to write down any encounters from the day and to consider if you are able to make a shift to a kinder response the next time you meet. It would also enable you to acknowledge yourself for meetings in which you rose above old behaviors and reached out with kindness. You might want to record how that felt, as you expressed kindness in a new way.

Walking a kindness path is different for each of us. We each get to walk it in our own way. Be kind to yourself on the journey. There are no rules, just opportunities to which you can respond or not. Either way, you're already adding kindness to a world that needs it.

Whether your intention is to have a more fulfilling life or just to have more fun on the journey, you are making a difference in the world.

We're grateful that you are on this journey with us.

With love from our hearts to yours,

*Pat and Larry*

## Who Do We Want to Be as a Community?
*Find the goodness in everyone
and pass it on with kindness.*
Dolly Parton

We are in the middle of a crisis. Throughout our country, we are seeing a dramatic increase in people who are experiencing homelessness. It is a reality that affects millions of people – those who are living without a home and those who encounter them in their daily lives.

This is a defining issue in our country. How we respond to it will tell us and tell the world who we are as a people.

### How did we get here?

In our city and throughout our country, this issue upsets the lives of many people. Most see it as an annoyance to be removed, not a larger problem to be solved. It is easy to understand their dilemma.

People don't know how to respond, so they don't want to think about what they may be called to do.

It is easy to turn away and to insist that unhoused people be removed so they do not have to deal with the issue. When confronted with failures of our social and economic systems, we don't want to acknowledge them.

If people are sleeping on the sidewalk in front of a business, the business owner fears that customers won't come, and their livelihood is at stake. Strange people wandering in neighborhoods cause residents to fear for the safety of their families. The presence of unhoused people alters the quality of life in a city.

It is easier to see them as an irritation in our lives rather than as people who deserve our consideration.

### Can we see them through a different lens

I invite you to consider the consequences in their lives. Can you see their humanity and realize that they deserve our compassion rather than our judgment?

Here in Asheville, city ordinances place responsibility for this disturbing situation on the people whose presence is upsetting to others.

Like many cities, Asheville has an ordinance against vagrancy. I looked up the definition of *vagrant*: *"a person who wanders about idly and has no permanent home or employment; an idle person without visible means of support."*

Wow! This definition covers everyone who is homeless and justifies removing them rather than helping them.

Is this how we want to resolve a complex issue that affects thousands of lives – by criminalizing people who are already struggling with overwhelming challenges?

I invite you to consider the consequences in their lives. Can you see their humanity and consider the difficult circumstances that they live with every day? We don't know the life stories that led them to the streets, and if we did, we would probably have more compassion and less judgment.

Can we see their innate worthiness as human beings?

**How did we get to this point?**

Many people still see a person without a home as defective in some way. Let's consider the underlying causes of the increased homelessness in our country.

During the last few years, our economy has suffered because of the restrictions in response to the Covid epidemic.

The COVID-19 pandemic and the resulting lockdown caused 114 million people to lose their jobs in 2020, and many others lost income due to reduced hours. Many families have not been able to recover and have lost their homes and/or suffered health problems related to the stress of the situation.

The economy has recovered, but that has not impacted everyone equally. Some people have been forced to sell their homes. In order to avoid foreclosure, many have had to accept a lower price than the value of their homes, and that has pushed them into the rental market, with rents going up dramatically in some areas.

Among the homeless population, many crises come together - multiple challenges which most of us do not have, including poverty, physical disability, mental illness and addiction.

In addition, they need to find a way to live without having a safe place to sleep, access to bathrooms and showers, food, clothing, or a way to wash clothes. Just surviving seems like a fulltime job.

**Mental health issues are still seen as a personal failure.**

People with mental health issues still carry a stigma and are seen as less worthy, rather than as fellow human beings who deserve consideration.

With less or no income, many have suffered from health problems for which they cannot afford health care. Then, the stresses of insecurity in their lives can lead to mental illness for which they cannot afford appropriate treatment.

Today, many unhoused people have some form of mental illness. Living on the street exacerbates existing problems for some people, and it causes mental illness in others.

The stresses of living without a home cause some people to seek temporary relief from challenges they are unable to meet. The lure of a drug can be very appealing. Then people become hooked into the hell of an addiction that takes over their life.

**Addiction is an illness, not a character flaw.**

Today, with so many addicted people showing up on our streets, it is easy to see them as irresponsible and lazy. Can we decide to see them as having a serious mental illness from which is difficult to recover?

Many people have one or more addictions. We have an opioid epidemic in our country, caused, in large part, by the marketing tactics of drug companies that have incentivized doctors to overprescribe highly addictive opiates. The results are showing up in our communities.

According to an article from *PsychCentral*, an important reason that the stigma against addiction still exists is the of lack of education around two key principles:

There are factors beyond a person's control that lead to substance use.

Brain changes result from substance use that make it difficult to stop.

Having known people who became easily addicted to a pain killer or casual drug use, I have seen the danger of that first use. Among people who are living with overwhelming stress, a little relief seems worth the risk.

**How are we willing to respond?**

Are we willing to see the innate worthiness of everyone we meet?

Father Greg Boyle is the founder of Homeboy Industries in Los Angeles, an organization that provides services to former gang members and returning ex-offenders, helping them to create successful, productive lives. He asks us to consider:

*Here is what we seek: a compassion that can stand in awe*

*at what the poor have to carry, rather than stand in judgment*
*at how they carry it.*

Are we able to do that?

Here, we are being called to look through a lens of compassion.

You do not need to volunteer with an organization that provides support for unhoused people, but that would expand your understanding of the challenges these people face. The most important gift you can give is to see the humanity of every person you may now be rejecting as not worthy.

You don't know their stories, and if you did, you might have compassion for them rather than judging them for how they appear to you now.

There are many things that can be done to provide appropriate responses to address this crisis in our communities. That is the subject of my next post. It all has to begin with how we see each other and who we, together, choose to be in this world.

**Who do you choose to be?**

Here, we are being called to look through a lens of compassion.

We ask you to consider whether you are able to expand your current view of people less fortunate than you are. It is not a requirement, just an opportunity.

We're grateful that you are on this journey with us.

With love from our hearts to yours,

*Pat and Larry*

# Awe and Wonder in Our Lives

*Sometimes we need to be taught how and where to seek wonder,*
*but it's always there, waiting, full of mystery and magic.*
Diane Ackerman

Do you need a break from discussions of serious matters that weigh heavily on your heart and mind?

During the last few weeks, I have felt myself experiencing sadness, frustration and a bit of overwhelm, as I considered the challenges around homelessness in our communities and the serious disconnect in our politics.

I needed to shift my attention to something uplifting – a respite of sorts – so I could get back to my usual positive mindset.

The easiest way that I know to do that is to be aware of the many things in my life that inspire awe and wonder. It's amazing how easily we forget to notice those things around us all the time that uplift us, if we would just notice them.

I thought a lot this week about experiences in my life when I had unexpected feelings of awe and wonder. The two most outstanding were in response to major natural events.

### The Power of Awe and Wonder in My Life

When I was in my early teens, I spent the summer as a "mother's helper" on Cape Cod. My duties included kitchen duties and helping to care for their four children. I enjoyed my time with them, and I especially appreciated the occasional time off.

One evening, I was out for a long walk in a still- undeveloped area. As twilight transitioned into night, the moon lit my way. At one point, the road went through a tunnel of trees. I could see that it was dark in that tunnel. I was fearful, as an innate self-protective impulse arose in me.

Not knowing what to do, I looked up at the sky and noticed the magnificent vastness and beauty of the heavens. I was awe-struck. I don't know how long I gazed in wonder, but I was outside of time. When I finally looked back at the road ahead of me, I realized that, in the vastness of the universe, I did not matter.

Amazingly, feeling insignificant was comforting. No longer afraid, I proceeded down the road and through the tunnel of trees.

I have carried the impact of that moment with me through my life. It is beyond my rational mind. Deep within me, I have a knowing that I am safe wherever I go.

Another experience occurred when I was a teenager. Our family was on a camping trip in Vermont. One evening, as dusk was descending on us, strange lights appeared in the sky – waves and ribbons of colored light. I had heard of the Northern Lights, but I had never anticipated seeing the aurora borealis.

My brothers and I laid on our backs and drank in the dancing motion of light above us. I was mesmerized. I was transported out of my body into the middle of the motion and colors, as if they were also around us.

No words can convey that experience. Awe and wonder are the closest I can come.

## Inviting Awe into Our Lives

Of course, we cannot wait for rare acts of nature to fill us with awe. All of nature inspires feelings of wonder and appreciation in me. I love hiking in the forest and sitting or standing by a waterfall. The closer, the better.

The ocean has an energy unlike any other. I'm not big on swimming behind the breakers, although I've done it many times. Larry and I enjoy walking barefoot, with saltwater caressing our feet. Breathing in the ocean air and wiggling our toes in the wet sand are enough to make me feel connected to the vastness of the ocean and to all of life.

Of course, nature is around us every day, wherever we are. When we shift our gaze from the large to the small, we have innumerable choices.

All of my life, I have been a collector of beautiful offerings from nature – seashells, colorful rocks, and seed pods to be used as part of our home décor. Spring flowers from desert trees, to be pressed until dry, then used on wall plaques or note paper. Even dried grasses that grow along the road look great in a large basket.

Of course, we don't have to take something home with us. Just a walk in a park or in our neighborhood offers plenty of beauty when we stop to observe it and appreciate it.

A Canada Goose family, with Papa watching over his brood, ready to chase off anyone who gets too close.

A spider, weaving her web in an intricate pattern designed to ensure that she has food for the day.

Squirrels delightfully chase each other, as if they, too, know the joy of play.

Butterflies and hummingbirds drink from deep within flowers, spreading pollen where it needs to go.

Birds singing their stories, looking for a mate or foraging food for a new family.

Beauty, beauty all around.

### Wonder All Around Us

We can experience wonder every day if we are so inclined. That is the choice that I made this week.

I considered the friends who showed up and offered help and the pleasure of their company.

I thought about the information that came to me, unasked, but in response to a need or a desire within me. Those synchronicities are as awe inspiring as any dramatic display of nature. They nurture a deep part of me and remind me that I am always cared for.

Yes I am in awe of our life – how easily it flows, even when challenges arise, which they often do.

We are so richly blessed, especially by friends and family, and by the realization that we have the privilege of living on Planet Earth at this time.

We have the privilege of being a voice of love and kindness at a time when the world needs all the love it can get. And we have the joy that comes with walking this chosen path.

We're so glad that you have chosen to join us on our journey, and we wish you joy and awe and wonder on your journey.

We're grateful that you are on this journey with us.

With love from our hearts to yours,

*Pat and Larry*

# New Opportunities to Spread Kindness

*Great opportunities to help others seldom come,
but small ones surround us every day.*
Sally Koch

Larry and I are always looking for opportunities to expand the reach of our kindness. It is not an unselfish act, because we benefit from it as much as anyone we encounter.

## Within Three Feet or So

Carrie Newcomer is one of our mentors, through her songs and words of wisdom. She sings of the unlimited ways to practice kindness "within three feet or so."

This has become a kind of mantra for us, as we consider how to expand our practice of kindness to include more people and in situations where we had not thought about the opportunities right under our noses.

As we discussed this idea, we realized that we were missing a lot of chances that show up every week. All it takes is a state of mind that is open, looking at people we encounter every day – at home and at work, as well as when we're out in our community.

## Expressing Gratitude

Gratitude is an important part of any kindness practice. We all like to be acknowledged. A simple "Thank you" or words of appreciation can uplift someone's day. They also uplift the person speaking the words. One benefit of gratitude is that everyone feels better because of it.

As we go through our day, we have many chances to make a sincere comment of appreciation. It might be acknowledging a nurse in a doctor's office who provided good care, or the person who puts out the produce in a grocery store. I often will say, "You're very good at what you do," or, a simple "Great job" as I notice the results of someone's efforts.

The key to expanding the reach of our kindness is paying attention and noticing whoever is in front of us. Even on the phone, when someone helps us as part of the routine of their day, a few kind words go a long way.

### In Your Family

We often assume that people in our family know that we love them. It's important to take a moment to acknowledge them and to express our gratitude for the little things that they do or just how much we appreciate having them in our life.

We all like to be acknowledged. A smile when someone walks in the room says it all. No words needed.

A simple "Thank you" makes a difference after someone has completed a chore. Even if a child or teenager does not do what we consider to be a great job, we can acknowledge what they did, before gently pointing out what still needs to be done.

The kindest thing we can do is to notice and engage with them. "How did your day go?" may lead to a conversation that reinforces your connection. If it is obvious that someone is upset, "Are you okay?" opens the door to offering support when they need it. "Do you want to talk about it?" might follow.

When we notice each other, we find many opportunities to nurture our relationships.

### At Work

Work environments vary greatly. Some are friendlier than others, but we can always add some kindness to any workplace.

Greeting people as we enter is the easiest place to start. Greeting them by name and saying a few words of acknowledgement starts the day on a positive note. It is helpful to relate to each other as they show up in the workplace, leaving politics or other issues that divide people outside.

When we're part of a team, we have additional opportunities to support and encourage each other. In team meetings and problem-solving sessions, we have a chance to listen to each other, to acknowledge their ideas, and to add our own as an addition to, rather than instead of their ideas.

We're grateful that you are on this journey with us.

With love from our hearts to yours,

*Pat and Larry*

# Nature as Part of Our Kindness Journey

*Those who contemplate the beauty of the earth
find reserves of strength that will endure
as long as life lasts.*
Rachel Carson

We have talked a lot about the importance of kindness in our daily lives and in the community. We have also talked about our vision for a kinder world, in which we live with love and kindness to one another.

We have not talked much about kindness to the world in which we live - the world that sustains us, even when we have not acknowledged the debt that we have to her.

Today, we are focusing on our gratitude and commitment to Mother Earth. We hope to raise awareness of our dependence on her and to inspire more appreciation for the gifts that she provides for us every day.

This week, in reading a blog post by Khanna Johnston of the Environmental Protection Agency (EPA), I was reminded of the important contribution that Rachel Carson made to our awareness that we must protect our environment from the poisons that threaten our very existence.

Rachel Carson was a marine biologist who, early in her career, focused on studying the ocean and its many inhabitants, then sharing her findings through a trilogy of books that became best sellers in the 1950s.

Her greatest contribution came later, through her concern about the threat to our environment caused by the increasing use of synthetic pesticides in the world. That led to her shifting the focus of her research to conservation.

Rachel's book, *Silent Spring*, presented the results of her research and that of other scientists who were concerned about damage from the use of pesticides. She predicted that, unless we stopped the poisoning of our planet, we would face a world without birds that would, eventually, be unable to sustain life.

The book was a bestseller, and it was a major factor in a growing awareness of the importance of protecting our environment. That led to a ban on DDT and other pesticides and eventually led to the creation of the U.S. Environmental Protection Agency (EPA).

Today, we are faced with an equally dangerous threat from Glyphosate and other chemicals used worldwide in agriculture. Many of our plant foods arrive full of chemicals that are toxic to our bodies. Equally important, the process of factory farming is depleting nutrients in the soil and poisoning the soil in which plants are grown.

## So, what can we do?

First, in order to protect ourselves and our families, we can buy produce locally whenever possible. Depending on where you live, you can take advantage of Farmers' Markets and/or a subscription plan with a local farm to receive a weekly supply of freshly harvested organic food.

Second, you can bring nature to you by growing some of your own food. A small plot in your yard or even a tiny garden on your balcony will supply more food than you think. The internet is full of ideas and instructions.

Another option is offered by the Tower Garden company. This aeroponic tower system can be used indoors or outdoors, and it produces nutrient rich food, using less water and less space than usual gardening methods.

Normally, I invite people to advocate for what they want. At this point, Monsanto and other big agriculture and chemical companies have bought law makers at all levels. I believe that our best way forward is to become less dependent on factory produced foods. I suggest that you take whatever action you can with #1 and #2.

## Spend more time with Nature

Above all, we encourage you to develop your relationship with Nature. Add time in nature to your weekly schedule and give it a high priority. You will benefit physically, emotionally and spiritually.

The more time you spend experiencing your connection with Nature, the more you will increase relaxation and peace in your life. As you do, you will develop more gratitude for all that Nature provides for us and expand your understanding of our interconnection with her.

We are much more likely to protect what we love.

We're grateful that you are on this journey with us.

With love from our hearts to yours,

*Pat and Larry*

# The Power of Patience on Our Kindness Journey

*Patience is not simply the ability to wait.*
*it's how we behave while we're waiting.*
Joyce Mayer

When we have a vision of something for our lives, we sometimes lose patience, wanting to see it show up now. That's understandable. But we need to be encouraged by the small steps that we are able to take as we live inspired by that vision in our daily lives.

We have imagined the world that we want to live in. It provides a foundation for our lives and for our kindness work, and we have developed daily practices inspired by that vision.

## Our Vision

Our vision is a world in which we live peacefully together with kindness and consideration for one another. We listen to others, so we can understand them rather than judge or condemn them because they have made different choices than we have. Love and compassion are the driving force in our individual interactions with one another and in the world.

Love in action shows up as kindness in our personal encounters – with family and friends, but also with strangers. It is considering their needs as well as our own, and taking action to support them in whatever way we can – whether with a smile and kind word in passing or an offer of more help where it is needed.

We believe that your vision is similar. If our visions are to become a reality on our planet, it will require major changes in the way that people feel about one another and interact with each other. We are all living in the present, and that vision seems impossible from where we are now.

Rather than feeling powerless, we can choose to look at it differently. We see that, in time, our combined visions can become a reality in the world if enough people choose to live their lives in harmony with them.

## This Requires Patience

No matter what anyone else is doing, we each can choose to live our lives in a way that models what we wish to see in the world. You may feel that nothing you do would make a difference, but we disagree.

We each have an impact on the small part of the world around us. Every act of kindness creates a ripple that goes out to other people, as the person who receives the kindness or observes it is inspired to pass it on to someone else.

We are energetic as well as physical beings. Everything that we feel or say or do radiates energy out to those around us. Scientists have demonstrated this phenomenon in several ways. This understanding has added a new dimension to the way that we think of the impact that we all have on other people. We now know that we affect them in a deeper way than we realized.

The changes that we want do not happen quickly, but they are possible if enough of us live the vision in our daily lives. We may not see the final transformation of the world in our lifetime, but we will have an impact on it.

We will see changes in our lives and in the lives of the people with whom we interact. We are all interconnected, whether we realize it or not. We are not just pieces in the puzzle of life. We are dynamic energy beings who have an influence on others wherever we go. Together, we are creating the world that we want to see.

What impact do you want to have? What do you want to add to the large picture of humanity? Take a few minutes and consider this question.

You have the power to begin today to live your vision in your life and to add it to the evolving new world that we are creating together.

We're grateful that you are on this journey with us.
With love from our hearts to yours,
*Pat and Larry*

# What Container Is Holding Your Life Experiences?

*Life is bristling with thorns, and I know no other remedy
than to cultivate one's garden.*
Voltaire

When we experience something in our lives that we prefer would not happen, we often feel sad, helpless, even angry at life. This week, I learned a new way of looking at these experiences.

In her article, "Stop Being a Glass - Become a Lake," Carrie Newcomer wrote about a lesson that she learned when her friend Gary Walters recounted an old story that he had heard.

A young apprentice went to his master and asked for help to deal with his deep sadness. The master told the apprentice to put a handful of salt in a glass of water, then drink it. The apprentice followed the instructions, then told the master that it tasted terrible – way too salty.

Then, the master walked with him to a nearby lake and told him to put a handful of salt in the lake. When the apprentice took a glass of water from the lake, it had no salt flavor.

The master took the hands of the apprentice and said to him, "The pain of life is pure salt; no more, no less. The amount of pain in life remains the same. But the amount we taste depends on the container we put it into."

Carrie said that the story was helpful for her. "My life may have its struggles, but there is still the light on the water, time working in the garden, walking with my dogs, chatting with my daughter. There is music and laughter, potlucks and fresh blackberries. There is poetry and birdsong, kindness, courage and decency."

This story spoke clearly to me, as well. Larry and I have talked a lot about what we fill our minds and hearts with every day. By expanding the size of our lake of feelings, beliefs and experiences, we provide a container for any pain or frustration that will hold them in waters of gratitude, love and the joy in being alive on Planet Earth at this moment.

Of course, we will sometimes have experiences that we wish we did not. Their impact on our lives will be largely determined by the mental company that they keep - the quality and frequency of our thoughts about them.

When we dwell on something unpleasant or painful, we add more power to that experience. When we notice things around us that enrich our lives or think about people we care about, we call in the power of love and gratitude. We are always adding to the size and content of our lake.

We all get to choose our container. Is it a container of frustration, annoyance and helplessness or a container of gratitude, optimism and joy? Whatever container we choose determines the quality of our experiences. Our life develops within the energy of the container that we carry within us.

As Carrie said, when the world has poured salt in her hand, "I can expand my sense of things, engage in life-giving activities and heart opening contemplation. I can hold unease or outrage in tension with love and grace, simultaneously and creatively."

So can we. Let's "Stop being a glass. Become a lake."

We are grateful to Carrie and Gary for this uplifting story.

We're grateful that you are on this journey with us.

With love from our hearts to yours,

*Pat and Larry*

# The Power of Our Questions

*Life is an unanswered question, but let's still believe
in the dignity and importance of the question.*
Tennessee Williams

We have several ways of thinking about life questions. One is to consider a large purpose for our life. "Why am I here?" "Is there something important for me to do with my life?"

The answer to that question may be elusive. If we are not able to see some specific reason for our life, we may settle on a broad concept such as to live a successful life or to live as a kind person. Then, with time, we fill in more details as our life unfolds.

Several years ago, I was inspired to a deeper contemplation of my life from a parable that I read.

## The Two Wolves

*An old Cherokee is teaching his grandson about life.*

*"There is this fight going on inside of me," he says to the boy.*

It is a terrible fight, and it is between two wolves.

One wolf is negative. He is anger, envy, sorrow, regret, greed, arrogance,

self-pity, guilt, resentment, inferiority, lies, false pride, superiority, and ego."

*He continued, "The other wolf is positive. – he is joy, peace, love, hope, serenity,*

*humility, kindness, benevolence, empathy, generosity, truth, compassion, and faith.*

*The same fight is going on inside you – and inside every other person, too."*

*The grandson thought about it for a minute and then asked his grandfather,*

*"Which wolf will win?"*

*The old Cherokee simply replied, "The one you feed."*

Now, as I go through my day, I notice what wolf I am feeding. I might feed the positive wolf at 9 am and realize that I am feeding the negative wolf later in the day, in the midst of all the challenges confronting me in that moment.

It's complicated. Some emotions and behaviors have become habitual. We react negatively to certain triggers, and we experience the same results every time. When that happens, we are unable to connect with others in a more positive way.

The wolf story invites us to make a conscious decision: which part of our nature do we want to dominate as we go through our lives. Most people would choose peace, love and joy.

That choice is easier to make than to express consistently in our daily lives. This brings us to the questions that we ask ourselves daily.

## The Importance of Daily Questions

We want to spend more time in the energy that supports our choice than the time that we spend having thoughts, words and actions that undermine that choice.

Perhaps the most powerful tool that we have to support our becoming more of who we want to be is questions that we ask ourselves every day. They will change from day-to-day, based on what is happening in our lives at that time.

Perhaps I am having difficulty in a relationship. The question for today might be, "How can I see my father in a different way today so that I will be kinder to him?" or "How can I connect in a supportive way with my father today?"

Perhaps I lose my temper with a family member who "pushes my buttons" with his thoughtless remarks. My question might be, "How can I stay at peace and allow my brother to be who he is without taking it personally?"

Perhaps I have begun to lose faith in my life path. I could ask myself, "Who can I talk with today or what can I read to get back to believing in myself?"

Every situation requires its own questions. With experience, we get better at asking helpful questions and listening, as we go through the day, for an answer to come to us. Answers often arise intuitively or from an idea that shows up in something that we read or hear.

I am often amazed at the synchronicities in my life, as information comes to me just when I need it. Over time, I have become better at noticing answers that appear in unexpected ways.

This whole process takes practice. It also empowers us. It offers us a way to have more control daily over the issues that are troubling us. They will change from day-to-day, based on what is happening in our lives at that time.

Remember to ask the most important question early every day. Then, be aware as you go through your day. Notice what shows up in front of you that may hold the answer you are asking for.

## The Other Side of the Coin
*Sometimes you need to question your answers*
### Alan Cohen

Most of us live with assumptions about our lives and about life in general. Those assumptions have solidified into beliefs that guide our daily choices and our judgments. Often, they are based on limited information, and they color our interactions with other people as well as how we view our own life.

I invite you to look at any beliefs that are guiding your life. If they are empowering, of course, keep them. If they are disempowering, making you feel less worthy of what you want for your life, or making you see other people in critical ways, I invite you to choose a different belief that supports you in living the life that you decided to live.

Some beliefs may make it more difficult for you to move beyond a challenge that you have in your life. What if you chose to let go of that belief? What if you chose a more empowering belief that enabled you to move through the challenge with confidence and grace? Would you be open to adopting that belief?

Question: "What belief is not serving me?" "What belief would empower me to become more of who I want to be?"

It may be helpful to find a friend who supports the changes you want to make or a group of people who support you and can offer their wisdom and encouragement. For many of us, this is a time to call on a higher power in our lives for guidance, then to listen as we go through our day.

With or without the help of other people, we truly are more powerful than we think we are. Question, "What can I do today to connect with the power within me?"

Now, be aware as you go through your day, and notice the wisdom that shows up for you.

We're grateful that you are on this journey with us.

With love from our hearts to yours,

*Pat and Larry*

## Why are Some People Invisible to Us?

*Open your heart—open it wide.*
*Someone is standing outside.*
Mary Engelbreit

We have spoken before about invisible people in our lives – people whom we pass and choose not to see. For many people, homeless folks fall into that category. For others, it may be people of color, people with disabilities, or people who look disheveled, who seem not to respect themselves enough to meet a certain standard of appearance.

We make silent judgments that it is easier to ignore them, not wanting to engage or not knowing how to engage. That is a big subject. Today, let's look a little closer at the invisible people in our personal lives.

**Who is standing outside my heart waiting to be invited in?**

Part of our kindness journey is identifying people in our personal lives who seem invisible - sometimes, even when physically present.

Have you had the experience of being a gathering of family or friends and you noticed that someone is left out of the discussion? That may be the choice of a quiet person, content to listen, not wanting to take part in the discussion. It might be fear of not having anything worthwhile to share. As a shy child, I experienced that.

Rather than ignoring a silent one, we could acknowledge them by inviting them into the conversation. Often that opens a door for them to participate. The response of the group is important at that point. Criticizing their idea or making fun of it is a sure way to prevent their sharing in the future. It requires us to be mindful of the needs of the person.

**Reaching Out Can Be Awkward**

The most common way to exclude someone is to ignore them completely. I have cousins whom I haven't seen or spoken with for many years.

In a case like this, you have both changed in the years that have passed. Is it possible that you can reconnect and find that you have enough in common on which to build a relationship? Perhaps happy family memories. Perhaps experiences that would be uplifting to share with each other. Perhaps books that mean a lot in your life or a video about a shared interest.

There are so many possibilities.

We can realize who else we have made invisible in our lives and decide to reach out. In many families and with old friends, that would be all it would take to reconnect. Our lives are busy. People have moved and not let people know. For some, a reconnection might mean a lot to them – and to you.

We could step up and acknowledge someone we had never spoken with. – perhaps a neighbor who never speaks to us. Some might respond to a smile and a kind comment. Others might not.

Our reaching out might lead to a pleasant relationship, one that includes smiles and greetings when we see each other, perhaps even more. We choose how we respond to them at our encounter, and they choose how to respond in return

**Part of kindness is respecting other people's choices.**

Reaching out doesn't always lead to a reconnection. I have an older brother who had a falling out with our family many decades ago. He has reappeared a few times at family gatherings, but little in between.

Years ago, he decided to ignore our younger brother, Bob, and me. I continued to call and leave a message on his birthday. No response. His choice.

Time to let go.

## Disconnect in a Family

Larry's experience was different. He was seven years older than his brother, Marshall. He was out of the family home while Marshall was in 5th grade. With their age difference and with Larry's busy sports schedule in high school, they were not close.

Although they did see each other infrequently at family gatherings, neither one reached out to make a deeper connection.

About 20 years ago, their cousin Mickie let Larry know that Marshall was dying. He encouraged Larry to visit him so they could reconnect. I was with them during that visit, and I saw how much it meant to both of them. A short time later, Marshall passed away. He was at peace.

Larry was at peace also. It was a healing to his heart that he did not realize that he needed.

### Who is waiting to be invited into your heart?

You probably won't know until you reach out to them and see their response. There might be a gift in it for both of you.

Let's make this fun!

We're grateful that you are on this journey with us.

With love from our hearts to yours,

*Pat and Larry*

## Pat's passing on 8/26/2023

Kind·ness
noun
Love with its workboots on

The love of my life, Pat, the writer of this blog, passed away on August 26th. Pat went into the hospital for a non-threatening condition and never came out.

Pat loved all of you and we wanted to share our journey on the kindness path, and invite each of you to walk your own kindness path. Pat's writings were inspired by her Divine muse and she practiced kindness, compassion, smiles, and encouragement daily.

There is so much to say about my relationship with my dearest Pat over the 22 plus years we were together. One phrase, unconditional love, expressed through kindness, joy, humor, awe and curiosity, and non-judgement; embodied Pat and her writings.

Our creating www.livingwithkindness.com was our greatest project together. We were also writing a book about the power of kindness, yet unfinished. My hope is that all of you will continue to walk your kindness path, and invite others to our blog.

Pat wrote her last blog post on August 18, 2023 in the hospital. I will try to keep the livingwithkindness.com website alive, as long as possible. I have found a couple wonderful folks, who are helping to work on publishing Pat's blog post, as a book on Amazon.

Thanks to all of you who are spreading kindness.

Love to all

Larry

# Acknowledgments

Thanks to everyone who helped work on making this book a reality. Special thanks to Dylann Rhea and Veronica Cavallaro. A very special thank you to Larry Downing, Pat's husband, who was the driving force to get this book created.

## About the Author

*"I have this crazy belief that there is a blessing in everything that shows up in my life. Often it is disguised as a burden or a tragedy, but in time, when I choose to notice, the gift presents itself to me."*

I am the mother of two wonderful grown children and grandmother of three. I am also a wife, daughter, sister, mother-in-law, aunt, cousin, niece, friend, colleague, neighbor and citizen. Every relationship has added to my understanding of myself and others – and whatever wisdom I have acquired has come through many failures as well as successes.

My husband, Larry, has been my constant companion for the last 22 years, and we have supported and encouraged each other on our kindness journey. One underlying theme of our life has been our desire for love to be the driving force in all our relationships. As a result, we have looked for ways to express love more fully and to see the intrinsic value in everyone we interact with. We have not always succeeded, but we are better at it now than we used to be.

From my heart,
Pat

# References

Pat Downing composed many incredible posts on her website, some of which could not fit into one book. To read more and learn about organizations that were close to Pat's heart, please visit www.livingwithkindness.com.

Made in the USA
Las Vegas, NV
18 December 2024

14710883R00215